HIGH PERFORMERS

Recruiting &
Retaining
Top Employees

Alan J. Dubinsky
Purdue University

Steven J. Skinner
University of Kentucky

THOMSON ™

SOUTH-WESTERN

Australia · Canada · Mexico · Singapore · Spain · United Kingdom · United States

High Performers: Recruiting & Retaining Top Employees
Alan J. Dubinsky, Steven J. Skinner

VP/Editorial Director:
Jack Calhoun

VP/Editor-in-Chief:
Dave Shaut

Acquisition Editor:
Steve Momper

Channel Manager, Retail:
Chris McNamee

Channel Manager, Professional:
Mark Linton

Production Manager:
Tricia Matthews Boies

Editor:
Kim Kusnerak

Manufacturing Manager:
Charlene Taylor

Production House:
electro-publishing

Sr. Design Project Manager:
Michelle Kunkler

Cover Designer:
Beckmeyer Design
Cincinnati, Ohio

Cover Image:
© Getty Images, Inc.

Printer:
Phonenix Book Technology
Hagerstown, MD

DEDICATION

To Caron and Elliott Dubinsky, David Bailey, Irene Rossman, and the memory of Frederick Manzara

To Moira, Aaron, and Carrie Skinner

Disclaimer

All of the employee activities discussed in this book are as told to us by those interviewed. Names of individuals have been changed, and names of organizations have been omitted, to protect the privacy of those who participated in our study.

TABLE OF CONTENTS

Preface

Have you ever wondered why some people do more than is expected of them? Have you ever wondered why some employees seem to do much more than is required of them while others do as little as possible? Have you ever wondered why some individuals can take a bad situation and turn it into a "winner"? Have you ever wondered why some employees, in the absence of any direct supervision, go beyond the call of duty, go the extra mile, exert extra effort? And have you ever wondered why some personnel don't step "outside the box" and are satisfied doing solely what their job description requires? Well, wonder no longer!

Through a series of interviews with close to two hundred employees from all kinds of organizations—large and small, profit and nonprofit—and in all kinds of positions—from the top of the organization to the bottom—we have identified 13 *drivers* that impel individuals to go beyond the call of duty, to walk the extra mile, to expend the extra effort. And what is particularly interesting is that while some individuals are driven by fame and fortune, others go the extra mile even though they know that their bosses will probably never find out that such meritorious behavior ever occurred. Regardless of the reasons for their going beyond the call of duty, however, we found that high-effort workers choose to engage in such activities at their own discretion, i.e., they are not mandated to do so.

So what drives these superstars? What leads them to go above and beyond the call of duty? In the following chapters, you will discover that some are simply motivated from within; that is, they find themselves in situations requiring special attention. Rather than asking their supervisor or peers for assistance, they seize the moment. Others respond to circumstances, and thus go the extra mile, owing to their work environment. Some workers' commitment to customer service drives them to excel. And still others jump at the chance to deal with a difficult situation simply to earn more money or to be promoted.

What is particularly intriguing about our findings is that those who go beyond the call of duty are not just those at high levels of an organization, nor are they the luminaries that we read about in the popular press. They don't need to be a Jack Welch, a Bill Gates, or a Carly Fiorina. They may well be the person with whom you carpool, your next-door neighbor, your office mate, or the organization's custodian. In fact, *you* may even be such a person!

This book is written for both managers and employees. It will give managers ideas about how to energize their workers to go the extra mile. And employees may well be so inspired from the anecdotes we describe that they discover their own ardor to go beyond the call of duty, to transcend their job description. In an era of increasingly keen competition, going beyond the call of duty or expending extra effort clearly is an approach for enhancing an organization's position in the marketplace—and it can be a cost-free one at that!

The core of this book focuses on the 13 drivers that induce employees to go beyond the call of duty. In Chapter 1 we introduce our study that led to our identifying the 13 drivers. Then, the drivers are detailed in separate chapters, each of which begins with actual illustrations from our study that clearly portray employees' going beyond the call of duty. In each situation, you will notice that the individual chose to take action voluntarily. Following the illustrations is our diagnosis of what drove these employees to engage in such meritorious efforts. Concluding each chapter is a prescription of how managers can recognize these drivers and foster exceptional performance with their employees.

So let's not waste any more time. After all, time is money. Let's begin our journey into how to get employees to go beyond the call of duty.

Beyond the Call of Duty:
I Don't Know What It Is,
But I Know It When I See It!

"You just set the work before the men and have them do it."
– Henry Ford

Some time ago, one of the authors was addressing a group of mid-level managers at a conference. The topic was developing a performance culture in the organization—one in which workers can bring the maximum amount of effort to their jobs. The talk began with a story about an air traveler who boarded a flight in Seattle on the way home to Lexington, Kentucky. On the Seattle-to-Portland leg, he snacked on peanuts; from Portland to Dallas, more peanuts followed. Because of time zone changes, more peanuts were served after he changed planes in Dallas bound for Atlanta.

While traveling from Dallas to Atlanta, the hungry traveler could taste the fresh popcorn he would buy in Atlanta before the final flight. But since the plane was late getting into Atlanta, he had no choice but to hurry to the gate, only to find the Lexington flight boarding. After he checked in, he ran to the snack area, only to find the popcorn machine closed.

Disappointed and desperately hungry, the passenger boarded the plane and took his seat. While the flight attendant asked him how his day had been, he said not bad considering he was starving. She informed him that she would be happy to get him some peanuts. He muttered something about popcorn and the fact that he had been craving it all the way from Dallas to Atlanta. Just as the airplane door was about to close, a gate agent ran into the plane with a bag of freshly popped microwave popcorn for the hungry passenger. It seems the flight attendant had phoned in an order from the plane.

In analyzing the incident, the speaker noted that the flight attendant had made a choice to go above and beyond the call of duty. He asked members of the audience to think about the incident and describe what had taken place—i.e., what drove the flight attendant to take it upon herself to provide the hungry passenger with a bag of microwave popcorn? Exactly what was *it* that would explain this behavior? At this point one member of the audience—visibly excited—jumped to her feet and said, "I don't know what *it* is, but I know *it* when I see it."

Each of us, at one time or another, probably has had an experience similar to that of our hungry traveler. Be it a doctor, teacher, accountant, or receptionist, we had a noteworthy experience. Maybe it even motivated us to write a letter to the company telling them what a terrific employee they had. In any event, it was an employee's performance that had a lasting impact on the customer and placed the organization in an extremely favorable light. It is what the speaker meant when he talked about workers bringing an unusual amount of effort into their jobs.

But questions remain: Why do employees do it? How can you explain the extra effort of the flight attendant? Was it done for pay or a promotion? Most of us are probably like the manager who couldn't explain the behavior but knew it when she saw it. Let's take a close look at the episode that began this chapter:

- The flight attendant made the decision to go the extra mile and order the popcorn for the hungry passenger.

- There was no manager present to instruct the flight attendant to order the popcorn; she made the decision on her own.

- Unless the passenger writes a letter to the airline, management may never be aware of the extra effort the flight attendant put forth.

- Even if management becomes aware of this incident, the flight attendant may not be directly rewarded for it.

Many different metaphors have been used to describe changes that have taken place in modern organizations: reengineering, paradigm shifting, and framing, to name a few. The emerging organizations have been described as lean, flexible, responsive, and perhaps above all else, highly competitive. These organizations are also characterized by a new type of employee, referred to by some as the knowledge or high-discretion worker. A major challenge facing organizations today—especially in this time of intense competition—is inspiring this new breed of high-discretion worker to *willingly* go beyond the call of duty when the circumstances call for it.

THE RESEARCH

This is not a book about managers. Rather, it is a book about workers, written for managers and workers alike. It is a book about employees who have gone above and beyond the call of duty in performing their jobs. When given an opportunity to go the extra mile, these workers voted "yes." The flight attendant could have just as easily voted "no" to getting the popcorn.

So why do workers do it? Why do some employees go the extra mile, while others do not? To answer these critical questions, we interviewed approximately two hundred employees in a variety of organizations—large and small. We interviewed nurses working in large hospitals, service reps in large companies, and cooks working in pizza parlors. We interviewed teachers, real estate agents, and wholesale salespeople. Workers from all levels in dozens of different types of organizations were asked about situations in which they had gone above and beyond the call of duty. The kinds of organizations in which our interviewees were employed, as well as the kinds of jobs they held, are presented in Table 1-1 and Table 1-2.

Table 1-1. Interviewees' Organization Types

Physical therapy	Fireplace and patio retailer
Landscape architecture	U.S. military
Industrial equipment manufacturer	Waste removal services
Hospital	Social service
Auto repair	Drafting
Energy	Discount retail sales
Elementary school	Religious school
High school	Real estate
Railroad	Wholesale distribution
Cell phone sales	Agricultural products
Clothing retailer	Marketing research services
Retail pharmacy	Toy retailer
Vacuum retailer	Employment agency
Bookstore	Telemarketing
Packaging and shipping service	Property management
Video rental	Chemical manufacturer
Financial services	Advertising agency
Health club	Bar
Restaurant	Seminar sales
Apartment complex	Newspaper
Optical shop	Computer manufacturer
Retail office supplier	Brokerage
Insurance agency	Direct marketing
Retail grocery	Tanning salon
Automobile manufacturer	Internet services
Appliance manufacturer	Book distributor
Construction	Race track
University	Hotel chain
Legal services	Discount home supply
School memorabilia manufacturer	Major league baseball
Airline	Golf course

Table 1-2. Interviewees' Job Types

Therapist	Pharmacy technician
Landscape architect	Design drafter
Customer service rep	Clerical
Nurse	Executive secretary
Automobile mechanic	Principal
Coal miner	Clergy
Proprietor	Real estate assistant
Teacher	Director
Chief engineer	Store manager
Railway brakeman	Administrative assistant
Sales manager	Vice president
Sales/marketing rep	Office manager
Retail sales	Insurance broker
Pharmacist	Plant coordinator
Assistant manager	Service manager
Laborer	Bartender
District manager	Restaurant waitperson
Bank teller	Accountant
Volunteer	Deputy director
General manager	Case manager
Cashier	Development coordinator
Leasing agent	Patient care manager
Manager	U.S. Army recruiter
Insurance agent	Research assistant
Communications consultant	International marketing coordinator
Branch manager	Account manager
Professor	Student teacher
Foreman	Staff support
Traffic manager	Project manager
Attorney	Purchasing agent
Aircraft mechanic	Marketing/sales intern
Driver	Risk manager
High school coach	Teacher's assistant
Dormitory security	Host
U.S. National Guard lieutenant	Chef's assistant
U.S. Army major	Restaurant busser
Cook	Supervisor
Youth basketball coach	Golf pro shop attendant

Specifically, interviewees were asked to recall an instance when they went above and beyond the call of duty in performing their job. The incident had to be one in which they—the workers—*solely* decided what had to be done and one in which their supervisor or management would not have a direct impact on their decision to perform. Also, the interviewees were asked to discuss the circumstances surrounding the experience. In addition, they were queried about what drove them to engage in the particular activity that represented their going the extra mile or beyond the call of duty (i.e., the reason for the special job behavior).

Our findings are insightful and go a long way toward answering the question posed earlier: Why do some workers go the extra mile? In short, we identified 13 reasons that explain why individuals are motivated to expend additional effort. Not every worker we interviewed was motivated by all 13 drivers. In fact, many of our interviewees suggested that only one of the drivers motivated them. But taken together, the next 13 chapters paint a composite picture of the worker who willingly decides to take action that requires going the extra mile, and provide managers with guidelines for recruiting and encouraging workers to rise to such high levels of effort when necessary.

2

Internal Motivation:
Gee, I Actually Get Paid to Do This?

*"There are three ingredients in a good life: learning, earning, and yearning." – **Christopher Morley***

Shawn is a part-time sales rep for a firm that markets graduation products and class rings. He sells to high schools and a few colleges. His office has seven other sales personnel. As a part-time employee, Shawn usually works six-hour days, leaving at 5:00 p.m. to be with his family. One late afternoon Shawn was wrapping up his day. He had taken care of several clients, attended to the requisite paperwork, and shipped several orders. Feeling great, he was about to exit when he heard grumbling in the office. Apparently, a huge mailing that was to have been sent out first thing the next morning had not even been started. The office staff looked confused and mortified for having forgotten to prepare the mailing. As they complained about their circumstances, Shawn said that he and his family would prepare the mailing at home that evening. Although there was no manager present to approve Shawn's actions, he believed that the situation warranted it. He called his wife, informed her of the family's "volunteer activity," and promised to pick up pizza on the way home as an incentive. The next day, the mailing went out right on schedule, and Shawn's boss exonerated him for not having received prior approval.

Amanda is an assistant to the vice president of a newspaper division who is responsible for the circulation of several newspapers around the United States. She has been asked to determine circulation projections for the newspaper. The company recently had sold a number of their tabloids, which meant that the current report on circulation numbers was no longer valid. Amanda could have used a shortcut to craft the report, as her division has a formula for making such calculations. The formula, though, was not precise. Her boss would have been satisfied with use of the shortcut, despite its potential inaccuracy. Amanda, however, decided to redo the entire report accurately and completely, even though she had several different projects going concurrently. This took her two extra days. The end result was that the division's database and the vice president's report reflected the most current and reliable data possible.

Phil, a junior in high school, had a summer job at a golf course. He loved playing golf, so being a maintenance worker on the course allowed him to play a lot of golf for free. Early in the summer, the golf course's junior golf program (for children 5–14 years of age) was about to begin. Suddenly, though, the person who was to plan and organize the program became very ill and had to take a leave of absence. There was no one else to take this person's position, and the golf pro (Phil's boss) was too overwhelmed with work to take on an extra responsibility. Without even thinking twice, Phil volunteered to take over the program as well as do his regular maintenance work. This was only his third year as an employee at the course, yet he thought that he could do the job (or is that jobs?). And do the job, he did. His boss was ecstatic about the great success of the youth program that summer. He was even happier about not having to hire and train someone special from outside the course to head up the program.

Ethel is an assistant property manager for a firm that manages several apartment complexes. Her job essentially involves marketing the complexes, visiting with prospective tenants, signing leases, assigning service tasks, and doing walk-throughs when a tenant has moved out. She is not responsible for performing any maintenance or service-related tasks. Frequently, tenants become irritated when something in their apartment is not functioning that is the responsibility of the property management firm (e.g., the air conditioning, the refrigerator, the electricity). One day, a tenant called and screamed about his faulty air conditioner. It was 90 degrees, the sky was clear, there was no breeze, and the humidity was high. He had called for the past three days, yet no repairperson had fixed the broken air conditioner. Ethel attempted to calm the hot, sweaty tenant and said that someone would be over shortly ("Yeah, sure," he said.). Ethel hung up the phone and called her service people; they were all attending to other tenants' problems. Although she was not required to do service work, she did have some skill with plumbing and heating systems. She thought: "What the heck; let's give it a try." She picked up a toolbox and then drove over to the "steaming" apartment. When the tenant opened his door, he asked: "Is this some kind of joke or what?" Ethel explained that she was there to try to get his air conditioning to work. She entered, examined the system, quickly identified the problem, and repaired it on the spot—all to the amazement of her "hot," disbelieving tenant!

DIAGNOSIS

Shawn, Amanda, Phil, and Ethel took charge of situations that required attention. None of them, however, *had* to take charge. Shawn could have gone home and enjoyed the evening with his family and not run the potential of incurring the anger of his boss. Amanda could have taken a shortcut approach to her assigned task (which would have been fine with her boss). Phil could have done solely golf course maintenance without the extra burden of running the youth golf program. And Ethel could have made the tenant wait until a service person could fix his air conditioning. Despite the inconvenience, despite their assigned duties and responsibilities, and despite management's expectations, all four of these high-energy people decided to do more than was required of them. And in all cases, the result was extremely favorable. What impelled these employees to seize the gauntlet was that they had a prodigious degree of *internal motivation.*

Certain employees are simply highly motivated. They have a high need for achievement, for success. They expend their energy in job-related pursuits that likely will be mutually beneficial for them and the firm. They create win-win situations (recall the results of the efforts of Shawn, Amanda, Phil, and Ethel). These kinds of individuals tend to be overachievers. They are like the Energizer Bunny®: "They keep going and going and going." And not only are they internally motivated, they receive a high degree of self-satisfaction from their job. Several of our interviewees expressed such traits:

- "I am motivated to have a job well done. I like to have my work be perfect." – Shawn, our school products salesperson

- "It's my personality. It's my internal drive that leads me to just come out and do more than is expected of me." – customer service rep, business machines firm

- "Personally, I have gotten a lot of satisfaction from doing more than I have to." – district human resources manager, large multinational toy chain

- "I always have had the internal motivation to do the best possible job that I know how; the satisfaction from the act is important to me." – Amanda, the newspaper assistant to the vice president

- "I am kind of a perfectionist—I like things to be done to their fullest." – Phil, our summer golf course employee

- "I have always been motivated to provide excellent service in whatever I do. I hate lazy people." – Ethel, the assistant property manager

- "I desire to do my job the best that I can." – MIS support specialist, bookstore

R$_X$ FOR MANAGERS

Motivated employees who receive tremendous satisfaction from their jobs are a manager's "riches." These individuals, just like our four protagonists above, usually need relatively little guidance, seek additional work, use creativity, and identify potential problems before they occur (as well as solutions to them). They aren't afraid to look at new ways to solve old problems or adapt the old ways to make them more effective and efficient. They run on a seemingly unending energy source. And believe it or not, managers can have an impact on this internal drive of theirs. How? Try the following:

RECRUITING

- Recruit employees who manifest high energy. Identifying this trait can be done using several standard psychological tests. It can also be done by asking candidates how they spend their time, how much time they expend at work, and what their goals are.

MANAGING

- Design jobs so that they have variety. Variety affords employees an opportunity to do a variety of different tasks.

- Create jobs that give employees feedback. Feedback lets employees know how well they are doing, so that they know what to continue doing and what to change.

RETAINING

- Provide jobs that offer employees autonomy. Autonomy offers employees job latitude, thus empowering them.

3

Initiative:
Sometimes Ya Just Do It!

"It takes time to be a success, but time is all it takes."
– Anonymous

Lindsay's a vault teller at a bank and trust company. Her job usually is fairly calm—even mundane. But one Saturday morning it was anything but that for her! Lindsay arrived at work to discover that at one of her firm's banks, the vault had been improperly set at closing time the night before. This translated into one of the bank's having almost no money on hand for business that morning. Therefore, the branch where Lindsay worked had to transfer thousands of dollars to the hapless branch. But who was going to do this? Lindsay volunteered with reckless abandon to transfer the money, and to do so in her own vehicle with no attendant (make that armed guard!) at her side. She gleefully scooped up the moneybag, drove to the other site, and delivered the money. Once she got back to her bank, she began to think of the potential consequences of her actions: "Oh my gosh, I could have been robbed." "I could have been in a car accident and sitting in the middle of traffic with thousands of dollars." "The money could have fallen out of the car door or window." Next time, Lindsay decided, she'd think more carefully before blurting out: "I'll do it!"

Roberto, a high school principal, realized that one of his seniors was one credit short of graduation. Now this wouldn't have been a problem if graduation weren't within one week! Unfortunately, the student was nowhere to be found in the school. Because seniors at Roberto's school are excused from classes the last week of the school year, the student had taken the day off—unaware of his one-credit deficiency. Roberto jumped into his car and drove to the student's house. He pounded at the door, rang the doorbell incessantly, and even yelled for the student—all to no avail. Roberto climbed back into his car and was about to leave when the student appeared, asking why Roberto was visiting his home. Roberto convinced the errant student to take care of the situation so that he could graduate. And everyone lived happily ever after: The student quickly arranged to make up the credit before graduation, and Roberto was proud that he had prevented a student from falling between the cracks!

Tom is a district field manager at a seed company, where he's worked for over 24 years. He's become well acquainted with many of his territory's customers. Planting season is a crucial time—farmers want their seed when they are ready to plant, not a minute later. As Tom says: "When it's time to plant, our guys hit it pretty hard. When the window of planting is open, they don't need to be held up. They need the seed to be there." One of Tom's farmer customers was preparing to plant the next day. The weather had been dicey for the past week, so the farmer was especially keen about planting immediately. The farmer wasn't expecting to receive the load of seed from the seed company until mid-morning of the next day. Nonetheless, Tom (who's salaried, not hourly) decided to surprise him. Tom went to the seed company's warehouse at midnight, loaded a truck with seed, and delivered it to the farmer's farm in the wee hours of the morning, thus allowing the farmer to get an earlier-than-expected start on the planting. After all, the farmer was counting on Tom to get the job done—even if he did so in the dark of night.

A guest had plans to stay in a hotel for a week. The first night at the bar, she became friendly with Mike, one of the hotel's bartenders. In fact, she mentioned to him that she planned to be a guest for the next seven nights. She also mentioned to Mike that she liked to drink a certain kind of herbal tea prior to going to bed, as it calmed her down and made her sleepy; the regular kind of tea would keep her awake. Now Mike, who's "only a bartender," decided to check to see if the hotel stocked the soporific tea. He couldn't find the prized tea, so he asked the manager on duty at the front desk whether it was available in the hotel's pantry. It wasn't, but soon it would be! After his shift had concluded, Mike went to the store to purchase the tea—enough for the guest's weeklong stay at the hotel.

A young foreign student died unexpectedly in the emergency room of a university hospital. His girlfriend was with him when he passed away, but both students' parents were home in China. The girlfriend, who was the closest person to the deceased, had no support system—she was all alone and feeling abandoned. Jodi, the hospital's "care manager," picked up the gauntlet and spent countless hours over the next few days with the distraught woman. During this time, Jodi contacted the campus international student association and the dean of students. When some friends of the deceased student arrived, Jodi helped them reach the young man's family, in addition to speaking with the Chinese embassy, assisting the medical examiner, talking with university officials and other agencies, and arranging for the deceased's parents (upon their arrival at the university) to speak with the health care providers who had cared for their son. Through Jodi's efforts, both the girlfriend and the parents were able to deal with the tragedy with greater ease.

DIAGNOSIS

The employees at a bank, a high school, a seed company, a bar in a hotel, and a university hospital all engaged in behaviors that went well beyond the call of duty. Their efforts, activities, and tasks were not part of their job descriptions nor required of them. Lindsay, Roberto, Tom, Mike, and Jodi didn't wait to be told what they should do in their respective situations. They seized the moment, they jumped at the chance, and they assumed roles that hadn't been designed specifically for them. But in each instance, the five employees focused on the needs of their "customers." They took special care to do so—and in each case, special care was requisite.

So what drove them to act? The abovementioned protagonists and many of our other interviewees report that they performed their "extra" duty as part of a philosophy that embraces the aphorism: "*Sometimes ya just do it.*" This means that waiting until the employee is instructed to act is inappropriate and smacks of ineptitude. Standing on the sidelines while the team is getting crushed makes no sense. To these individuals, walking the extra mile simply is prudent. The words of some of our "Herculean employees" speak volumes about the reason for their special behavior:

- "We just kind of naturally do it." – book clerk, small bookstore

- "It was a nice thing to do; I always see a job that has to be done—so I just come in and do it." – district manager, a large video chain

- "I just kind of step up to be in charge." – officer, National Guard

- "This is part of my job." – Roberto, our high school principal

- "You need to do it." – Tom, the seed company sales manager

- "This is my normal habit of being a working person and manager." – manager, property management company

- "I thought that there was something that I should do." – Mike, our bartender

- "It's what we all should expect of ourselves, regardless of performance standards." – deputy director, medical center

- "There is a zero defections policy in the military. You must accomplish the mission to 100 percent completion." – recruiter, U.S. Army

- "It's the logical thing to do." – international marketing coordinator, seminar firm

- "There was more work to be done and a deadline to meet." – manager, retail clothing store

- "Everyone was extremely busy, so why ask the manager to go do it when I can do it." – server, restaurant

R_X FOR MANAGERS

Employees often face challenges or circumstances that require special discretionary effort on their part. Not all will seize the opportunity, however. Some employees will pick up the gauntlet, they will identify things that they believe they "should" do on the job, and they aren't reluctant to take charge. Of course, for such performance to occur, the work environment must be right and the employees' perception of the situation must be on target. So, what's a manager to do? Try the following:

RECRUITING

- Ask applicants for examples of projects that they initiated on their own. Alternatively, ask what have they done to improve the processes or procedures on jobs they have held.

MANAGING

- Empower employees to take action when they have the opportunity to do so. Don't penalize them, though, if they make mistakes. Rather, use errors as a learning device for your "Herculean" employees. Empowering employees but chastising them for slipping up is a great way to disempower them.

- Identify areas in your business where problems are likely to arise and alert employees to those areas. Instruct employees to take corrective action when such situations arise, even if it involves taking a "calculated" risk.

- Model the "sometimes ya just do it" behavior for employees. After all, why should they engage in such behavior if you don't practice it? They shouldn't—and won't!

RETAINING

- Explain the benefits of practicing "sometimes ya just do it" activities to your employees, as well as the downside of not practicing it.

4

Upbringing:
A Chip off the Old Block

*"What the mother sings to the cradle goes all the way down to the coffin." – **Harriet Ward Beecher***

Nathan, a customer service rep, arrived at work one morning on tenterhooks. A group of environmental engineers from China was coming to see an engine that they had ordered from Nathan's firm—a large industrial products manufacturer. The Chinese engineers wanted to examine whether there were any problems with the engine, because a previously purchased engine had missing parts. "Would everything be ready for them?" wondered Nathan. "We can't afford to rile them again." Well, everything wasn't ready! In fact, by the time the engineers arrived, the engine had *already* been packed and sent to the shipyard, 15 miles from the plant. It was late in the workday—after Nathan had technically concluded his work; he was not allowed to receive overtime pay. Instead of passing blame or asking someone else to attend to the engineers, however, Nathan sprang into action. He drove the Chinese visitors the 15 miles to the dock, asked some of the shipyard workers to open the box containing the engine, and then made a detailed examination of the engine—part-by-part—with his Chinese customers. All parts were accounted for and present! And to top off his day, Nathan took the group on an evening sightseeing tour of the city. The end result of this customer service rep's efforts? The engineers were ecstatic about their good fortune and have become a major account for Nathan's company.

Mai-Lin is a teacher at a public school. Teachers are expected to be at work between the hours of 7:30 a.m. and 4:00 p.m. Well, Mai-Lin often surpasses such expectations. Once each academic term, Mai-Lin holds conferences with students' parents. These confabs are an important aspect of a student's academic growth and development and are taken seriously by Mai-Lin. Conferences begin at noon and typically last until 8:30 p.m., or even beyond—well after the designated ending work time for the teachers. Mai-Lin's efforts accommodate parents who cannot attend a conference until after their workday has concluded. This behavior occurs four times a year, three days in a row for each of the academic terms. Clearly, the conference schedule is an inconvenience to Mai-Lin, but she keeps doing it nevertheless.

Joe works for a large railroad company as a brakeman. The job's tasks require rapt attention to detail. Joe arrived on the third shift one evening (a midnight to 8:00 a.m. stretch). He and his partner (a friend of his) were responsible for 16 different tracks that night. Well, his partner's wife had given birth three days earlier. During those three days, the partner had been away from his job taking care of his wife, the new baby, and the family's other two children. He was exhausted from his familial duties, as he hadn't slept much in four nights. Joe knew that his partner wasn't prepared to do his job, as he could hardly keep his eyes open, much less work effectively. So, Joe invited his pal to take a snooze—which he did for the entire eight-hour shift! During that time, Joe did double duty, performing the work of two people rather than one.

Dave, a store manager for a tractor distributor, observed a man who looked dispirited. He approached the individual and asked if he could assist him. The man then went into a litany about how poorly Dave's firm had served him. The man had ordered a new engine from Dave's company for his tractor, but it didn't work— it kept dying shortly after it was started. The man was demanding an immediate replacement. It was planting season, and time was of the essence. Unfortunately, an alternate engine was not to be found in the warehouse or at the factory. To salvage the sale and to attend to this farmer's needs, Dave got on the "horn," calling all-around until he found the right motor. Then he jumped into his truck, drove two hours to pick it up, drove back to his store, got the engine up and running, installed it in the customer's tractor, and then drove the tractor over to the customer's farm. What a wild and wooly period this was for Dave!

DIAGNOSIS

The foregoing vignettes are suggestive of employees who willingly go beyond the call of duty. Nathan, Mai-Lin, and Dave worked hard to keep their customers happy, satisfied, accommodated. And Joe allowed a sleep-deprived friend to catch up on his rest. In each instance, these individuals did more than was expected of them in relation to their job descriptions. In fact, Nathan was "off the clock" when he expended his efforts, as was Mai-Lin to some extent. And Joe probably would have gotten into trouble if his boss had learned that he did the work of two people on a job that required extremely close attention. What moved these people, each in their own respective job situations, to engage in such meritorious behavior? There is an underlying reason that ties these four individuals together.

The common theme that energized these employees to walk the extra mile is *upbringing*. Childhood is a strong predictor of future behavior—on and off the job. Watching and listening to one's parents or guardians over time can instill in an individual a blueprint for life that can be difficult to change, at least in the short run. Parents who take on more and more responsibility on the job, perform extensive volunteer work, or take on additional duties in the home leave an indelible impression on their kids. Their example will likely encourage their children to behave in similar ways. Words from the foregoing employees, as well as other interviewees, clearly reflect this credo:

- "I do more because this is kind of the way I was brought up."
  – Nathan, our customer service rep

- "My parents did such things." – employee, landscaping firm

- "The way I was brought up as a child has influenced what I do now." – Mai-Lin, the school teacher

- "I just learned from my father that time is not the important thing—friends and good work are the important things."
  – vice president, coal company

- "A lot of my job behavior has to do with the way I was raised by my dad, and what he instilled in me growing up." – Joe, our railroad brakeman

- "If you're from an honest background, you just do the right thing."– Dave, the tractor supply sales manager

Do the "right" thing, indeed!

R$_x$ FOR MANAGERS

Children observe the behavior of their family members. Some witness extensive effort-intensive activities that are unusual, that are beyond the norm. Others observe mediocrity or indolence. Individuals whose parents taught them to take action, to do something, to take charge are people who likely will go beyond the call of duty as employees. Clues to this kind of philosophy and job demeanor can be discerned prior to hiring the individual. How? Try the following:

RECRUITING

- Scrutinize the job application to see how applicants spend their time. Do they idle away the hours or are they enthusiastic and involved in many activities, job-related and otherwise?

- Ask applicants about their backgrounds and how they spent their time when growing up. Did they spend endless hours watching TV or playing videogames, or were they actively involved in a variety of energy-laden pursuits?

- Ask applicants what beliefs were instilled in them as they grew up. Do they mention that there was nothing in particular, or were they taught to engage in activities that require going beyond the call of duty?

- Ask applicants to mention an incident when they went beyond the call of duty as a child and what led them to do so. Do they bring up their background as a reason?

- Ask applicants about some of the key lessons they learned as they were growing up. Do they describe helping others or expending additional effort?

5

Self-Satisfaction:
It's Spelled P-R-I-D-E

"A man cannot be comfortable without his own approval."
– Mark Twain

Ben is a carpenter foreman for a construction company. He works Monday through Friday and is salaried. His job entails handling some paperwork, making sure the construction jobs are moving along smoothly, ensuring that each site has the right amount of materials, and dealing with homeowners or customers. It was Friday afternoon, almost time for Ben to depart for the weekend and for his lake cabin. During that day, one of his subcontractors had been cutting holes in the front of Ben's brick office building for window placement. Because the subcontractor was behind on the job, he informed Ben that he planned to continue cutting the holes until sundown and on Saturday. Ben thought for a moment about his weekend and the cabin and then informed the subcontractor he would be there with him. Ben thought that it was necessary to get the windows in as soon as possible to keep out the elements and ensure that no unfortunate individual fell out an open window hole.

Nancy, a research assistant at a medical center research laboratory, was preparing to leave for the day. It was 5:00 p.m., she was tired, and all of her co-workers were gone. As Nancy walked out of her office and down the hallway, a research scientist implored her to help with an experiment. The experiment was time sensitive, and the scientist couldn't wait until the next workday. One of Nancy's co-workers was assigned to work with this particular scientist, not Nancy. In fact, Nancy worked with another scientist in the lab. Without hesitating, Nancy said "yes" to the scientist's request for help. The experiment was a success, but it required Nancy's staying three extra hours to provide the assistance.

J.T. is a salesperson for an outdoor furniture and hot tub retail outlet. Although much of the business is walk-in trade, frequently J.T. must leave the store to call on customers. For example, not long ago he drove to a customer's house on a weeknight ("off the clock") to make an estimate on the purchase of a hot tub and patio furniture. The negotiations lasted over three hours, but he did make the sale. Then, when the time came to deliver the goods, as well as install the hot tub and assemble the furniture, the crew where J.T. works was backed up for two weeks. Consequently, he had to make all the arrangements to have the hot tub installed (including getting the gravel for the hot tub's base and calling an electrician), ensuring that it was functioning properly, and assembling the furniture. All of these activities took precious selling time away from J.T., and some of them were even performed in the evening and on a weekend (again, "off the clock").

Sara was assigned to contract a company that would paint all the offices in the large insurance company where she worked. As an office coordinator, such an assignment was part of her job. The way she ultimately got the painting job done, though, clearly wasn't. She called several painting firms, and each one informed her that they were booked up for at least one week. Unfortunately, her boss said that the painting had to be done by next Monday, five days away, when important customers would be visiting the office. With no paint crew in sight, Sara decided to recruit seven of her friends from work (and herself, naturally!) to do the painting on the weekend. Sara and her crew started early on Saturday morning, worked late into Saturday night, began again early on Sunday morning, and finished the job around 10:00 p.m. on Sunday, with time to spare before the arrival of Monday's guests!

Diagnosis

Notice the kinds of jobs in which our foregoing employees engaged. Ben is a carpenter foreman and attends to construction sites. Nancy is a research assistant helping research scientists. J.T.

is in sales at a retail outlet. And Sara is an office coordinator at a large firm. Many people may view such positions as a means to an end. Nonetheless, the individuals occupying these positions did not perceive their roles in this fashion. Rather, they seized the moment, went out of their way, walked the extra mile—when such efforts would not receive immediate monetary return. For these four people, their jobs weren't merely a job; they were much more. This group, as well as some of the other interviewees, took great pride in what they did, and *pride* is what impelled them to take their meritorious actions.

Pride is something one feels. It is a sense one has that says: "I succeeded; great job; nicely done." It can occur for the slightest of things or for something truly major. When an employee possesses pride, it makes him or her feel good, energized, happy, satisfied. And aren't these things that you want from your employees? Of course! Consider the striking statements that reflect the pride our interviewees feel for their extra efforts:

- "I don't look at dollar signs when I see someone [a customer]. My goal...is to know that I am doing right."
  – J.T., our retail salesperson

- "I did not want to see the program fail; it would have been costly to my organization if it did." – medical professor, university hospital

- "The scientist had no one else to help her; I take pride in what I do, whenever it happens on the job." – Nancy, the research assistant

- "I decided to go ahead and do it myself because I thought it was important to have our place presentable." – Sara, our office coordinator

- "I want to feel good about what I'm doing at work."
  – director of communications and development, nonprofit organization

- "I don't work just to make money. You have to like what you do. A lot of it boils down to the pride that you take in the work that you do." – Ben, the carpenter foreman

R_X FOR MANAGERS

Many employees want to take pride in what they do, as well as be proud about where they work. As noted earlier, pride produces good feelings in employees—their self-esteem, self-respect, and self-confidence increase. With such favorable emotions, employees are likely to take on additional responsibilities. Of course, pride is something that is generated internally—the employee either feels it or not. Nevertheless, pride is something that managers can help foster. How? Try the following:

RECRUITING

- When interviewing job candidates, determine whether pride motivates them. Is pride one of their hot buttons? Ask them to describe various job situations in which they have found themselves, and ask them what led them to take the particular action they did. Did any of the reasons have to do with pride?

MANAGING

- When employees ask for guidance, be sure to provide them enough latitude to solve the problem themselves. This will not only augment their pride when they arrive at the solution, but it will also enhance their problem-solving skills.

- Illustrate to employees how critical their job is to the organization. No matter whether a job entails rocket science or not, it still plays a key role in your organization. If it doesn't, then why do you staff it? You shouldn't!

RETAINING

- Let employees know that their job isn't just a means to an end (receiving their compensation), but that, done well, it can be a major source of self-satisfaction.

Empathy:
Walk a Mile in My Shoes

"A wise and an understanding heart." – 1 Kings 3:12

Kay, a student nurse in a hospital, was working alone on her shift, as is often the case. After all, she's expected to pick up the tools of the trade partly through instruction and partly through observation. Recently, she was left to her own devices, as her hospital unit was understaffed, and the patient census was unusually high. The end of the shift was imminent, and many of the nurses' aides were scheduled to depart for the day. Unfortunately, several of the patients had not yet received their baths. As the aides hustled to bathe the patients, Kay noticed that they were not going to leave on time because so many patients still needed baths. Plus, the aides were grumbling that once again they would have to leave work late. Given the situation, Kay took it upon herself to help bathe the patients. As a result, by the end of the shift, all of the patients had received their baths, and the aides were able to leave work on time.

Tim is a manager at a pizza restaurant. One Friday night, four servers failed to show up for work. What typically would have seemed like a busy period now seemed overwhelming. Patrons were irritated that they weren't getting served promptly, servers were grousing about their indolent and disloyal peers, more customers kept streaming in the door, and the delivery people were screaming for their pizzas. Here was a really bad situation that seemed to be getting worse as each minute passed. Tim decided to make the most (money, as it turned out!) of a bad situation. He gathered his four employees and placed them where they excelled, including sending two servers to the lobby to attend to the lines of customers. And as his employees executed their assigned tasks, Tim went into the kitchen and prepared several plates of breadsticks and filled glasses with soft drinks for his patrons to consume while they waited to be served. Tim's efforts defused the customers' disquiet and the four servers' angst.

Keisha was working her shift as a sales associate for a medium-sized retail department store chain when she noticed an elderly gentleman leaning on a table filled with sweaters. The customer was having difficulty holding himself upright, but he seemed intent on scrutinizing the merchandise. Keisha approached him, asked if he would like some assistance, and then proceeded to sell him three sweaters, two shirts, and a belt. The customer paid for the merchandise and was about to leave with his packages when Keisha asked him if he would like some assistance to his car. The man gratefully answered "yes." While her department peers staffed the department, Keisha almost carried the customer to his automobile ("he had all his body weight on me as I braced him while we walked"). Keisha put the gentleman in his car and then listened to his stories for over thirty minutes. At the end, the customer profusely thanked Keisha for her extra assistance.

Jon, an office assistant at a small screen-printing and trophy shop, was busily working one early Friday afternoon. He tried to ignore it, but he couldn't help noticing the tension that had been permeating the firm the past week. Employees were anxious, tempers were on the surface seemingly ready to explode, and customers' orders were backing up. Everyone, including Jon, was inundated. Just the most minute interruption or request could set off the whole staff. Jon knew that the weekend was fast approaching, but no one seemed to be looking forward to it. And he also knew that if the stress level in the company did not dissipate, it was likely to rear its ugly head on Monday—and thus resume where it had left off. In an attempt to defuse the situation, Jon raced out of the office, drove to a grocery store, and purchased soda, pretzels, and peanuts for the group back at work. Upon his return, he quickly arranged the "party," for which he received loud applause and cheering. The next Monday the staff returned to work from the weekend—and so did the employees' traditional calm and professionalism.

DIAGNOSIS

Kay, Tim, Keisha, and Jon each encountered distinctly different situations in their respective work environments. Two of the situations resulted in performing activities that attended to *both* peer employees and customers (Kay and Tim); one circumstance helped a customer feel extremely grateful and probably special (Keisha); and another effort dealt with relieving the discomfort of peers (Jon). They each observed a problem that might have gotten out of hand and have had unfavorable consequences. So they decided to take action. They did this on their own without asking for approval or advice. The result of their "extra" duties was salutary; in fact, the ends outweighed the means.

The people in these vignettes felt obliged to act because of their *empathy*. They saw a situation and took action because they understood what it is like to be on the other side (and we don't mean beyond the shining light!). They had been in a similar situation and didn't like it, or they had the finely honed ability to perceive things from the other person's shoes. Walking in someone else's shoes—being empathic—led our four individuals to solve a problem, thus keeping the ship on course. Reflecting on the words of some of our interviewees is extremely instructive, as it reveals their work value system:

- "I know what it feels like when that happens to me, so I don't like the other people [nurses' aides] to be left behind."
  – Kay, our student nurse

- "I know how it is...so if I can do a little bit more...they [customers] are going to function better." – manager, optical outlet

- "I did what I did because this is what I would want to happen if I faced similar circumstances." – patient care provider, large public hospital

- "I remember when I didn't have help as a resident, I didn't like it. So I make sure that residents in my unit don't experience what I did." – anesthesiologist, large hospital

- "I could see what my customers were experiencing. So I wanted to do something for them that would make them feel better." – Tim, the pizza restaurant manager

- "I felt that the student was really lonely, and I could relate to that." – teacher/advisor, boarding school

- "I knew how I would feel in that situation and therefore knew what my student would need." – teaching assistant, large state university

- "I will be old someday, and I hope that someone goes the extra mile for me." – Keisha, our sales associate

R$_X$ FOR MANAGERS

By putting oneself in another's situation, an individual can sense how he or she might feel if the tables were turned. With sufficient empathy, employees can be moved to take action—expend extra effort—so that the other aggrieved or discomfited person(s) senses an improvement. Employees who are empathic are likely to provide unsolicited assistance in a way that is neither intrusive nor demeaning. So what can a manager do to foster empathy among employees? Try the following:

RECRUITING

- Recruit individuals who demonstrate empathy. Several standardized psychological tests can be given to prospective employees to discern their degree of empathy. Check out your local library under the "psychology" section to find such scales and how to administer them.

- Ask applicants about the various kinds of activities, especially avocations, in which they engage. Those who volunteer in activities that benefit the community or society (e.g., answering a crisis hot line, visiting residents in a nursing home, spending time with a senior citizen weekly, coaching a Boys Club team) are likely to possess empathy.

MANAGING

- Provide empathy training through role-playing exercises. One's skill in empathy can be enhanced (you CAN teach an old dog new tricks) through skill development. Don't quickly assume that because an employee is not empathic that he or she has no hope.

- Exhibit empathy with employees and other parties.

RETAINING

- Explain the advantages of being empathic to employees. Let them know that empathy not only is valuable in their job, but it is also beneficial in every kind of relationship they have. In essence, it is a valuable characteristic that is transportable across numerous situations.

7

Concern:
When You Care Enough
to Do the Very Best

"It is well to remember that the entire population of the universe, with one trifling exception, is composed of others."
– John Andrew Holmes

Don arrived at work early one morning. As an OB-GYN at a large hospital, he didn't foresee any unusual deliveries. As he perused the charts, everything looked like a routine day—each expectant mother was doing well, and there didn't seem to be any rush. Then, he came across one chart that troubled him. One expectant mother was in labor—and was due to have quadruplets. The issue of quadruplets would have been difficult enough for Don, but there was an added complication: The woman had respiratory problems. Don made his rounds and saw his patients. When he came upon the woman expecting quadruplets, he noticed that she appeared to be in the very last stage of labor. He called to a nurse to get the mother to the delivery room, and he rushed to scrub and put on his hospital garb. He delivered the four infants without incident; mother and children were fine. As he completed his work and was about to depart, Don's patient suddenly went into respiratory failure and was rushed to the intensive care unit. She stayed there for six days. Don also stayed in the hospital for all six days, sleeping two hours a day. He was by her side during most of that time, and was there when she recovered.

Paula works as an assistant manager for a large retail chain. Her typical duties during her 12-hour shifts entail ensuring that merchandise is in stock and on the racks or shelves, helping department managers execute their jobs effectively and efficiently, training new sales associates, and working with customers. Paula was completing her shift one day, musing about the fun that she would have that night going to a rock concert with friends and then out for drinks afterwards. As she prepared to leave, the assistant manager who was to relieve Paula called and said that she could not come to work; an emergency had happened that required her attention. Paula still could have gone home; after all, the store manager would be on duty, if necessary. Despite the impending enjoyment, Paula volunteered to stay the extra shift—another 12 hours of work, for a grand total of 24 for her workday!

It was New Year's Eve, and things were popping at one of the locations of a national theme restaurant chain. Revelers were making merry, eating heartily, and blowing horns. The old year was about to end, and the new was about to begin. Well, as this went on, Jonathan, one of the establishment's servers, was about to encounter a problem that could have reached epic proportions. On the way to one of his assigned tables, a patron came up to him and carped about the absence of toilet paper and paper towels in the men's and women's bathrooms (how the patron knew that both bathrooms were paper deficient is unknown!). Jonathan went to the storage room but was unable to find any of the precious goods. He was dumbfounded: "How could we be out of this stuff on our busiest night of the year?" Rather than complain about the situation, he decided to take action into his own hands. Every employee was busy, even the managers. So, he raced outside, went down one block and entered a discount store, and purchased a sufficient quantity of toilet paper and paper towels for the rest of the evening. He thus eliminated the circumstances from becoming messy!

Mona has taught English, writing, and grammar in high school for 18 years. Most of the other teachers in these courses tend to give the students light workloads. Very little written work is done by the students in those other classes. Occasionally, they must prepare a one- or two-page paper, but no major written work is ever required of them. This has been the trend in Mona's school for the past ten years. Mona, though, does not follow what the other teachers are doing. Instead, she assigns ten-page research papers to each student in her three senior writing classes—for a total of 90 papers that require Mona's detailed examination. Former students often visit her after their freshman year in college is over to tell Mona that her research paper assignment was extremely beneficial to them in their first year in college. As a result, Mona is not about to relinquish this important assignment. It does require more work on her part, especially compared to her peers. But Mona is convinced that this is the right thing to do—going beyond the call of duty.

DIAGNOSIS

A physician, a retail store assistant manager, a restaurant server, and a high school teacher reviewed the conditions facing them and decided that they did not like what they saw. They believed that they should do more than what was expected of them in their assigned jobs. They somehow didn't feel right about dropping the ball or letting someone else do what they considered to be their job. They were driven to expend the extra effort, to go the extra mile, when doing so would have consequences. What drove them to such heights was a *concern* for others.

Don, Paula, Jonathan, and Mona manifested a deep concern for people, be they a patient, other employees, customers, or students. Each, in his or her own way, decided to do something extra on the job so certain individuals could receive special treatment—or in these four protagonists' eyes, the "right and deserved" treatment. Don couldn't abandon his patient; she had four new children to attend to. Paula didn't want to inconvenience her store manager. Jonathan wanted his customers to have a good experience, especially on New Year's Eve. And Mona just "knows" that she must train her charges well so that they will succeed later in life. These four people, along with other interviewees, felt a pledge to those whom they were serving, as the following quotations evidence:

- "I felt sorry for the customer; she needed to know that someone was there for her in case something happened."
  – manager, retail fashion shop

- "I felt responsible for her, as I was the only high-risk OB-GYN in town." – Don, our physician

- "I was able to make my boss's job easier."– assistant, real estate firm

- "I wanted to take the burden off my already stressed co-workers." – Paula, the assistant store manager

- "This was a college-bound group, and they needed to know how to write well." – Mona, our high school teacher

- "I just like to help people and take care of them." – owner, vacuum cleaner retail shop

- "My peers and my company are counting on me." – driver, multinational delivery service

- "Everyone was extremely busy. So rather than bother them, I decided to do it." – Jonathan, the restaurant server

- "I like to do things for others, as I care about others." – quality assurance person, restaurant

R_X FOR MANAGERS

Many people say that they are concerned about others. But are they REALLY concerned? Only if they truly manifest the behavior. It's one thing to say: "I care about you." It's another thing to show it. Just ask any person who's ever been in a relationship! Showing concern for others—whether management, peer employees, or customers—can go a long way toward engendering good feelings in the people being cared for. So what can management do to try to foster such caring among its employees in order to get them to go the extra mile? Try the following:

RECRUITING

- During the interview process, set up job scenarios and ask candidates how they would solve the situations. The illustrations should entail the possible expression of caring as a solution.

- Ask interviewees the value they place on caring and concern, why they feel this way, and how they have displayed this disposition in various settings. The lip service recruit will quickly be revealed.

- Recruit people who volunteer in activities that require caring and concern and/or are in jobs that require it.

MANAGING

- Practice caring and concern as a manager. Remember: Role modeling can leave an indelible impression on employees.

RETAINING

- Encourage employees to become involved in some volunteer effort. They may apply some of these new experiences to their jobs.

8

Reciprocity:
I'll Scratch Your Back
if You Scratch Mine

"What you get free costs too much." – Jean Anouilh

Charlene, a sales associate for a multinational discount chain, was working in the toy department during and immediately after the Christmas season. Over a four-week period, a customer kept coming into the department to find a PlayStation® 2 for his son. Continuously, the customer was turned away, as there was no PlayStation 2 available in the store (as supplies had been limited by the manufacturer). Not only was the parent unable to give his son the toy as a Christmas gift, but now it seemed as if he would never be able to give it to him, period. Charlene noticed the disgruntled and unhappy look on the customer's face each time he left without his bounty. Finally, one day a PlayStation 2 arrived! Charlene wrapped it up using four fifty-footer plastic bags, then placed it in a discreet location where other store employees would not find it. She placed a call quickly to the customer telling him of his good fortune. The customer made a beeline for the store and at last exited it with a big grin on his face. Undoubtedly, his son had an even bigger grin later that evening!

Deion has worked for several years as a support person in a large do-it-yourself national chain. He assists customers in finding the correct items they need in remodeling or redecorating their homes. One day, a customer approached him and berated Deion, Deion's employer, and the toilet that he had purchased from the store a week previously. A sales clerk had assured the customer that the toilet fixture would fit in the space available in the man's guest bathroom; after he got it home, though, he discovered that it was too big for the space. The customer almost became unglued—he shouted profanities and other invectives, waved his arms furiously, and threatened a lawsuit, all in a boisterous, hectoring tone. Deion, who is a hefty 250-pound former high school wrestler, did not cower at the customer's histrionics. Rather, he waited until the truculent, aggrieved customer had calmed down a bit. Then, Deion politely apologized for the problem and the inconvenience, offered to refund the customer his money for the incorrect toilet, and proposed giving him a 30 percent discount off the price of the correct toilet. The angry customer's eyes popped wide open in disbelief, his bristling demeanor ceased, and he graciously accepted the offer.

C.W. works in a large state university dormitory during the "graveyard" shift—8:00 p.m. to 8:00 a.m. She checks IDs to make sure that only residents are entering the dorm. She plays a quasi-security role. Well, one morning (bright and early, naturally), C.W. was preparing to end her shift when she received a phone call. The person who was to relieve her (and do the 8:00 a.m. to 4:00 p.m. shift) was running late and would be unable to be there before 10:00 a.m., two hours later than expected. C.W. was exhausted. She hadn't slept in 26 hours; plus, she had to study for an upcoming exam. She thought about discussing the situation with her manager or rapidly trying to find a substitute for the extra two hours. She longed to sleep, and the need to study for the exam was pulling at her. Rather than talking to her manager and ascribing blame for the situation or seeking a substitute, however, C.W. chose to "gut" it out, extend her shift by two hours, and then engage in sleep after 28 hours!

Jeff does inside sales for a wood products distributor. The products are chiefly for use in building or remodeling homes. Typically, customers either call in the orders, fax them, or come into the distributor's showroom. Rarely does Jeff go outside to attend to a customer. One Friday afternoon, though, just before quitting time, Jeff received a phone call from a concerned customer. The customer had ordered two outside doors for his new home, but the contractor had not yet installed them. And they wouldn't be installed until Monday, as the contractor took weekends off. The customer told Jeff that he had just moved some things into the house today, and planned to do so tomorrow as well, under the assumption that the doors would be installed by the end of the day—thus making the house contents safe from thieves. The customer asked Jeff in a very concerned tone what he should do. Jeff, who has extensive skill in working on houses, thought a minute and then said: "I'm about to leave work for the weekend. Why don't I just come over shortly and put on the doors? This way you can feel comfortable about the safety of the contents in your new house." An inside salesperson turned carpenter saved the day!

DIAGNOSIS

Charlene, Deion, C.W., and Jeff scrutinized the situations confronting them. They decided to do something unusual, even unexpected. Arguably, they didn't have to opt for the courses of action they took. Charlene could have allowed the parent to get the PlayStation 2 whenever it was in stock and the parent happened to show up. Deion could have simply refunded the malcontent's money and not offered him a discount. C.W. could have carped about her replacement's ineptitude or sought a replacement. And Jeff could have said: "Gee, that's too bad" to the worried customer. Yet none of these individuals chose the easy way out. They went out of their way, pushing the frontiers of *merely* acceptable employee behavior.

Each of these four individuals, as well as several other interviewees, engaged in their special behavior because they subscribe to the notion of *reciprocity*. Specifically, they believe that their job demeanor, especially that which is particularly commendable, is their way of "paying back" their respective firms for the manner in which they are treated. They go beyond the call of duty because their organizations treat them well: with respect, with adequate pay for the jobs they hold, and with a sense of family. They receive fair treatment from their firm and wish to treat the firm similarly. The pronouncements of some of our interviewees highlight the notion of reciprocity:

- "The people that I work for have taken very good care of me, and I feel like I should do the same for them." – Jeff, our inside salesperson from the wood products distributor

- "If you're treated well [by your company], you're likely to go above and beyond the call of duty for them."
  – customer service rep, large industrial products producer

- "Most of my employers have been very fine people, so I've wanted to do a great job for them." – chief engineer, multinational oil company

- "My boss is a super nice guy. He'd do just about anything for you as long as he could to help you out; so I'm just kind of returning the favor." – employee, large railroad

- "Dorm management has been very good employers; they've been very fair with me. I feel a part of the organization, so I just had to do this." – C.W., our university dorm attendant

- "My company takes care of its employees, so I take care of its customers." – Deion, the support person from the do-it-yourself retail chain

- "My philosophy is 'I do unto others as they do unto me.'"
  – Charlene, our sales associate from the multinational discount chain

- "My organization pays my salary, and they need me to be successful." – associate director, social service agency

R$_X$ for Managers

The treatment of employees can play a critical role in how employees act in their jobs—and thus their effectiveness. Employees want to feel that they are being treated professionally, uniquely, and fairly in their organizations. Such perceptions can provide the incentive for employees to perform at levels or engage in activities that are beyond acceptable performance standards. The preceding illustrations, as well as the attendant quotations, embody how appropriate on-the-job treatment from employers can have a marked impact on employees. After all, you can only expect employees to treat customers as well as they are treated. So how should management treat its employees? Try the following:

MANAGING

- When disagreements between you and employees arise, talk them out; don't shout them out. Histrionics are better left to the stage and movies.

- Treat employees with the utmost of respect. Whatever their job titles and roles might be, they have a job to do. Don't make light of it; in fact, applaud their work.

- Treat employees like the adults they are, not the children that some parental supervisors think they are. Teenagers are not adults and may require special treatment. But most employees are adults—and thus deserve to be treated accordingly.

RETAINING

- Clearly inform employees what you are providing them and why. And always deliver news—good or bad—in a professional and caring manner. Doing so may help foster a bond between the organization and your employees.

9

Customer Acquisition and Retention:
Ka-Ching, Ka-Ching, Ka-Ching

"When you've got them by their wallets, their hearts and minds will follow." – Fern Naito

---

Dave is a salesperson at a retail furniture store, a sole proprietorship. He typically is an in-store salesperson, awaiting customers to walk into the store. Recently, a customer called Dave's firm and was complaining about an expensive desk she had purchased a week previously. She was demanding that someone either come to her home and repair the defective desk (one of the drawers was sticking), or the store could take the defective desk back and refund her money. Usually, the store's service department attends to such issues; however, all service personnel were out making service calls. Although Dave had not actually sold the desk to the unhappy customer, he volunteered to go out and attend to the problem. So he drove to the customer's home, assessed the problem, and quickly repaired it, as well as the dissatisfied customer's mood and perceptions of the furniture store.

One of Mario's potential clients was flying all the way in from Ireland to evaluate a seminar given by Mario's firm. Mario is the international marketing coordinator for a leadership seminar firm. After viewing the seminar, the potential client would then decide whether his company would benefit by having its personnel attend the seminar. Mario picked up the guest at the airport, dropped him off at the hotel, picked him up the next morning for the seminar, took him to dinner after the seminar was concluded (spending his own money without receiving any reimbursement), discussed the seminar with his guest, showed him around the city, and then finally dropped the tired Irishman back at his hotel. The following day Mario picked up the potential client and dropped him off at the airport, but not before the potential client became a client by signing up his firm to attend the seminar he had seen the day before!

Gina is a sales associate at a major multinational discount chain. One day a customer came into Gina's department complaining that he had just purchased a computer desk from her department, was having difficulty assembling it, and as a result had broken two pieces of it. The customer wanted to return the desk and receive a refund because of the complications he was experiencing. The customer had just moved to the city in which Gina's store was located and didn't have the proper tools to work on it. In fact, he lived only two blocks from the store (as luck would have it—the store's luck, that is!). The unhappy customer worked many hours as a computer specialist and had little leisure time—most of which was currently being devoted to the troublesome assembly of the desk. After speaking with the aggrieved customer, Gina approached her manager with a solution: Gina volunteered to assemble a new desk in the store, deliver it the two blocks to the customer's apartment, and bring the other desk back for an exchange. The manager, amazed at Gina's idea and altruism, quickly approved her request. Gina's efforts led to the customer's returning a few days later and purchasing a computer chair and supplies for his desk.

DIAGNOSIS

Our furniture salesperson, our seminar international marketing coordinator, and our sales associate faced interesting situations. Dave faced a situation where the client's demands had to be met or else she was going to return the product and get a refund. Think of the ill will that may have been generated had Dave not volunteered to attend to a service-related task, something that was beyond his purview. Mario spent a considerable amount of time, as well as his own money, to woo a potential client; much of Mario's time was "off the clock," and he never did get reimbursed for his entertainment expense. He did, though, land a new customer. And Gina saved the day for her company by coming up with an ingenious idea that entailed her performing tasks that sales associates do not do at her store. The result for her was an extremely happy boss and customer; plus, the customer purchased additional items shortly after the potential fiasco. What becomes clear from the foregoing vignettes is that each of these individuals transcended his or her job boundaries for the purpose of either *retaining business* or *generating new business*, or both.

Customers are the lifeblood of any organization. Treat them well and they are likely to keep coming back for more, plus telling others about their success as a customer. Treat them badly, however, and their wrath can come down upon you (remember Charlton Heston in the "Ten Commandments"?). Treating customers badly will likely cause them to stop patronizing your firm, as well as to tell others (usually many others) about their unpleasant shopping experience. Our aforementioned savvy employees decided quickly to take it upon themselves to solve a problem rather than rely on others to do so, even if doing so resulted in their going well beyond the call of duty, and in the case of Mario, expending his own personal resources. All three of them knew, or at least had a hunch about, what needed to be done—and their efforts worked like a charm. Contemplate the following quotations from our interviewees regarding the reasons behind their actions:

- "If I do well by you and if I'm honest with you, you will tell your friends, and they are likely to tell other friends and acquaintances; that's how I build up the business."
  – Dave, our furniture salesperson

- "I was motivated by the simple fact that I wanted a client in Ireland." – Mario, the seminar marketing person

- "I did what I did because I wanted to develop a long-term customer relationship, and I knew that he would be a returning customer since he lived two blocks away."
  – Gina, our sales associate

- "If I do a good job, the client is likely to call my firm and ask me to do another job for them." – employee, landscaping firm

- "My helping a customer with a product that he or she didn't buy at my firm may lead that person to return at some point and buy something from me." – manager, cellular phone company

R_X FOR MANAGERS

Employees who go beyond the call of duty often realize that their extra efforts will likely improve their organization's business or external perceptions. Increasing business and the bottom line are critical employee goals. And assisting a disappointed customer can lead to favorable word-of-mouth promotion about your firm—and subsequent business from the formerly unhappy customer and that person's family and friends. Thus, getting employees to go the extra mile should be a major concern of managers. What can you do to generate this behavior from employees? Try the following:

MANAGING

- Clearly illustrate to employees how they fit into the organization's picture and the impact they have on the bottom line or the organization's goals.

- Show employees that you really care about customers— therefore, model respect toward customers.

- Provide examples of the kinds of job behavior that can engender customer satisfaction and loyalty. Do so using incidents from your own employees (i.e., make it realistic to them).

RETAINING

- Inform employees about the importance of satisfying customers and making them loyal customers.

10

Customer Satisfaction: Rubber Ball, Come Bouncing Back to Me

*"Make happy those who are near, and those who are far will come." – **Chinese proverb***

J.B. is an aircraft mechanic for a medium-sized airline. His job entails performing routine checks that are done on a regular basis as well as non-routine activities. Often, the non-routine tasks pertain to examining and repairing a part or system of the plane after its allowable duration of use has expired (e.g., three days, five days, etc.). If the usage time period for a part or system has elapsed, the plane cannot be flown until the repair has been made. Well, one night J.B. arrived for his eight-hour shift at 11:00 p.m. A plane had landed and was scheduled to depart at 6:30 the next morning. This meant that J.B. had little time to get the plane prepared for liftoff; he didn't want to ground the plane, since doing so would create logistics problems for the airline (e.g., delay other flights awaiting the arrival of this plane), as well as garner the rancor of J.B.'s boss. Unfortunately, not only did routine maintenance need to be done to the aircraft, but also one of its three-day systems was due to be replaced—a lengthy task. As the clocked ticked down toward the departure time, J.B. scrambled into action. He knew that his time was precious, that a major task lay ahead of him, and that he had to get the plane in tip-top condition. To accomplish his tasks, J.B. decided to forgo his two 15-minute breaks and his 45-minute lunch period; all of these are granted to mechanics by the union contract. He chose to forsake one hour and fifteen minutes of personal downtime to ensure that the plane would depart as scheduled—and indeed it did. J.B. watched as the flight took off, and then he headed for home and a well-deserved rest.

Rick has the assigned position as the retail sales manager and plant coordinator of a landscaping and garden supply firm. His varied tasks, though, don't always align consistently with those roles. Take the day—oops, night—that Rick had to become Jeff Gordon to ensure that a landscaping job would be started and completed on time the next day. As his regular workday ended, Rick received a call at 9:00 p.m. from one of his foremen. The foreman informed Rick that a job that was to begin the next day at 8:00 a.m. was short several trees and shrubs. As luck would have it, the requisite plants were not in stock. In fact, they weren't even available in town. Quickly, Rick got on the phone and called his contacts in the region. He found everything he needed at two different locations: one was 100 miles from Rick's store; and the other, 150 miles from the first site—which in turn was 200 miles from Rick's. Rick clambered into a truck and drove fast and furiously to the sources of supply. By 6:00 a.m. he had delivered the trees and shrubs to the job site, two hours early!

Jill was working her evening shift as a host at a popular local restaurant. It was 10:00 p.m., a usually quiet time for this establishment. In fact, the manager had let several of the cooks and servers go for the evening. All of a sudden, a group of 30 people walked into the restaurant hoping to be served. The restaurant was in no position to handle that many people—but it did, and it did so well, thanks to Jill's efforts. The manager essentially abdicated his role and offered no additional serving help; he just overlooked the difficult situation. So Jill sprang into action. After seating the large party (her host role), she quickly provided free snacks and soft drinks (a managerial role), provided help in the kitchen (a kitchen duty role), and assisted in taking and serving the group's orders (a serving role). What is notable is that Jill performed three extra roles (management, kitchen, and server support) that were outside her purview as a host. None of these efforts was expected of her nor even contemplated by her, her manager, or her peers. Nonetheless, she took on the assignments when she saw a problem brewing.

Jamie is a sales associate for a tanning salon. She basically ensures that all tanning booths are ready for each customer and attempts to sell them tanning supplies and products. One day a regular customer came into the salon. She entered a tanning booth and then realized that she had forgotten her $60 bottle of lotion. She didn't want to buy a sample of the lotion, as she had previously purchased a large bottle of it from Jamie's salon. To rectify the situation, Jamie offered the customer the use of her lotion. After her tanning session was over, the customer elatedly went over to Jamie, thanked her for the lotion, and told her that she "loved" the lotion. Jamie said to the customer: "Keep it; it's yours." Did Jamie have to loan her lotion to the customer? Did she have to give it to the customer? Obviously not—but she chose to do so—making the customer extremely happy.

DIAGNOSIS

An airplane mechanic, a retail store manager, a restaurant host, and a tanning salon sales associate went beyond the call of duty. One might say that their roles don't conjure up images of grandeur, pomp, or status. Nonetheless, J.B., Rick, Jill, and Jamie displayed behavior that made a significant difference to customers, and ultimately to their respective employers. Time was of the essence for J.B., Rick, and Jill; so they leapt into a problem-solving mode despite the inconvenience it caused them. And Jamie relinquished her lotion when she could have tried to sell a sample to the customer. These four individuals assumed the mantle, did more than they had to, with favorable results.

Why did these four employees choose the path they took? After all, they did not need to do the things they did. Well, they sought to solve a problem in order to *maintain customer satisfaction*—or even enhance it. Augmenting customer satisfaction can lead to customer loyalty. When customers are satisfied, they continue to make additional purchases—they come back for more. And if they are completely satisfied, they become hard-core loyal patrons. A patron's observing and/or receiving unexpectedly great service is a sight to behold. Hallmark service can be engendered through employees' going beyond the call of duty. Many firms realize that their *raison d'être* is to satisfy customers. J.B., Rick, Jill, and Jamie obviously do as well! The comments of some of our interviewees reveal this motivation:

- "We stay until 8:30 p.m. in order to accommodate parents who cannot come in earlier to talk with us about their children." – teacher, elementary school

- "Our mission…is to take better care of our clients than anyone else in town. It's fun to be able to provide a different level of customer service than what people are normally expecting." – agent, insurance company

- "I went ahead and took care of my customer because she IS my customer." – department manager, large discount chain

- "If I don't get the plane fixed on time, then a domino effect sets in. That plane and flyers are late leaving, which means subsequent departures and flyers on that plane will be late the rest of the day." – J.B., our aircraft mechanic

- "I like being able to provide a service that when clients use us and get to know me, they realize that I am ready to give them my best effort each and every time." – owner, employment agency

- "We want to make customers happy." – bartender, hotel

- "It's the right thing to do—it serves the customer."
  – case manager, large public hospital

- "I want her [the customer] to always feel like a special client."
  – Jamie, the tanning salon employee

- "I love to see the smile of a happy customer." – cashier, national fast-food restaurant

R$_X$ FOR MANAGERS

Customer satisfaction is the juggernaut and watchword that most firms embrace today. Some, unfortunately, give it only lip service. Others, thankfully, focus on it with all of their might. A means of generating a high level of customer satisfaction is through employees' efforts to go beyond the call of duty. As customers become more and more demanding, such efforts may become the essential element of business. As we witnessed in this chapter's vignettes, employees at all levels and in all kinds of positions can and are willing to engage in such exemplary behavior. So what can a manager do to foster a customer satisfaction mantra among its employees? Try the following:

MANAGING

- Have an incentive program that rewards employees for engaging in extraordinary behavior that satisfies customers.

- Empower employees to take action that can provide a high level of service. Give them the discretion to act along with the attendant organizational resources.

- Ask employees what makes *them* satisfied customers. Then indicate to them that such behaviors are likely to have a similar impact on your customers.

RETAINING

- Educate employees about the importance of generating customer satisfaction and the critical role they have in garnering it. Illustrate to them how high levels of service can retain customers and pick up new ones.

11

Role Modeling and Organizational Culture:
A Picture Paints a Thousand Words

*"You need three things in the theatre—the play, the actors, and the audience, and each must give something." – **Kenneth Haigh***

Lupe, a loan officer at a credit union, is about to close up shop for the day. It's 5:45 p.m., long after the designated quitting time of 5:00 p.m. A customer comes through the drive-through window, stops his automobile, and doesn't leave. Lupe, through the microphone, asks him what he needs. The customer tells Lupe that he needs $500 from his account to bail his son out of jail. Now Lupe realizes that she could send him to another branch that is still open; after all, it's time for her to leave, to take her personal time and attend to herself. Instead, she decides to open the money drawer and issue him the $500 that he so earnestly requires. Did Lupe have to do this? No! But she chose to do so, thus in essence reopening the credit union for one more transaction.

Iris, a drive-through cashier at a multinational fast-food chain, hears a cacophony outside. Patrons are driving up to the drive-through window and not getting any service; so they are honking their horns. The line is getting longer and longer—and the din is getting louder. Suddenly, Iris notices that the drive-through speaker is not functioning, so their orders cannot be taken. (Why the drive-through server didn't realize this is a mystery!) Iris seized the moment and went outside in a pouring rain to take the customers' orders. Then, she ran back into the restaurant and gave the kitchen the customers' requests. Iris's efforts kept the drive-through line moving. Basically, Iris saw a problem and took action, although she did not have to do so—least of all in a rainstorm.

Joel is a pharmacist and director of clinical services for a small family pharmacy. The pharmacy, unlike its large competitors, is open only during "regular" business hours: 9:00 a.m. to 5:00 p.m. Monday through Friday, and 9:00 a.m. until noon on Saturdays. To compete with the bigger pharmacies in the area, though, Joel's employer uses a beeper service that allows them to fill prescriptions in an emergency; rarely, though, does the beeper go off. Well, one Saturday night at 11:00 p.m., Joel is getting into bed when the beeper *goes off.* Bleary eyed and tired, he responds to the beeper. A customer has gone to the emergency room and needs medication. So, Joel climbs into his car, races to the pharmacy, fills out the forms, discusses the medication with the customer, and dispenses it to her. By the time he gets home, it's after midnight. Joel could have ignored the beeper and snuggled into his bed for a good night's sleep. After all, the customer wouldn't have known that the beeper signal was received, nor would have Joel's boss. Yet he didn't shirk his responsibility to the pharmacy nor to his customer.

Duane coaches a youth basketball team; he has an eight-game season. He is required to coach a one-hour practice one day a week (during a weeknight) and one game a week on Saturdays. Basically, his responsibility is to teach third- and fourth-graders the fundamentals of the sport: how to play the game and to execute plays. The very last practice of the season was upon him. As Duane had concluded his team's practice, he noticed that another team's coach had failed to show up for that team's practice. Rather than take his leave, Duane chose to coach their practice—and he did so in the same fashion as he does with his team. He ran that team's members up and down the floor, drilling them, having them play one-on-one, and guiding them where to position themselves in various situations. After the practice, everyone on that team gave him a high-five. From that point on, whenever they would see Duane, they would cheerfully greet him, slap high-fives, and talk with him at length.

DIAGNOSIS

A credit union employee, a fast-food cashier, a pharmacist, and a youth basketball coach all manifested behavior that was not required of them. All four faced distinctly different situations that were nettlesome to those on the "other side of the fence." Yet, each identified the problem and sought to take corrective action when he or she could have easily attended to his or her own personal needs and welfare instead. Lupe, Iris, Joel, and Duane expended additional effort when it was not in their self-interest to do so; ignoring the situation would have caused them no inconvenience. And customers and management would have never known the difference.

So what energized these four individuals to take charge, to embrace and solve the problem at hand, to do what was outside the bounds of their job description? The answer lies in *role modeling* and *organizational culture*. Management in Lupe, Iris, and Joel's firms espouses and role-models "going the extra mile" for customers. The firms try to treat their customers as being part of a family; doing so sometimes requires going out of the way for them (just as a parent does for a child). And Duane wanted to role-model extra-effort behavior for his and the other team— thus demonstrating to team members that sometimes one must do something special or go out of the way to help others. After all, third- and fourth-graders are very impressionable, so why not teach them a lesson beyond merely basketball? Organizations steeped in a value system that reflects "beyond the call of duty" behavior tend to practice what they preach at all levels. Why? Because this manner of behavior is modeled for employees by their managers, and it filters down to the lower ranks. This creed has been embraced by several of our interviewees, as attested to by the following statements:

- "Our managers always exhibit and encourage such behavior."
  – Iris, our fast-food cashier

- "I'm a manager, so I have to instill such behavior in my employees." – general manager, health club

- "I want to be a positive influence; I want the teachers and staff to regard me as a good principal." – minister of education, church school

- "I respect my boss, and I know that he works hard."
  – manager, pizza restaurant

- "We believe that you're not a customer here, but that you are a member—and that is continuously promulgated to us by management." – Lupe, the credit union loan officer

- "Management has really high performance standards, and we're in the public eye; it's something that we can be proud of." – driver, large multinational delivery service

- "Someday, I want to own a pharmacy and model it after my employer's." – Joel, our pharmacist

- "I wanted to show the kids that I was approachable so that they'd be approachable." – Duane, the basketball coach

R$_X$ FOR MANAGERS

Role modeling has been shown to be a very effective means of getting employees to change their behavior (or to continue the modeled behavior). It's also a method to get your employees to "buy into" your company's value system. If employees believe that management practices what it preaches, they are likely to follow suit. Moreover, an organizational culture that is favorable and permeates all levels of the organization (from the top down), can lead your employees to internalize what your firm stands for. The foregoing examples and subsequent quotations from interviewees illustrate what management can do through role modeling and organizational culture to get employees to go beyond what is expected of them. So how can managers accomplish this? Try the following:

MANAGING

- Regularly demonstrate/role-model the kind of behavior that you want employees to manifest: "If you show it, they will do it."

- Assign each new employee a "mentor" to help those individuals adopt the desired behaviors.

- Don't give mere lip service to employees' "going the extra mile." Employees are quick to discover a fake who does not practice or believe in his or her mantra. They rapidly reject the suggestion out of hand.

- And remember: Avoid modeling inappropriate behavior, as employees are likely to adopt it (e.g., "Gee, if the boss screams at customers, I guess I can at times, too").

RETAINING

- Don't practice a "Do as I say, not as I do" philosophy. Employees are quick to ignore such pronouncements. After all, why should they do something different just because you are the boss? They shouldn't—and won't.

12

Recognition:
Looking Goooooood!

"Glory is fleeting, but obscurity is forever." – **Napoleon Bonaparte**

Keith works for an environmental waste firm. The company removes hazardous and nonhazardous waste, cleans up methamphetamine labs, and eliminates lead and asbestos. (Clearly, Keith is in a "hazardous" job!) One day, Keith was assigned to clean an underground fuel oil tank at a gas station. Unfortunately, Keith's firm did not have the proper lifting and lowering devices with which to do the job. Also, the fumes that would be swirling around Keith's head could be dizzying, and the residue in the tank could get on Keith's skin unless he was careful. Because Keith did not have the appropriate lifting and lowering devices, he could have rejected the job. And in fact, management even informs its employees that owing to the hazardous nature of their work, they can decline an assignment because of safety concerns. Nonetheless, rather than decline the duty, Keith went into the tank, cleaned it without incident, and made his boss and a customer happy.

Karen is a proposal support coordinator for a printing manufacturer. Her job entails writing/answering requests for proposals (RFPs). One Monday around noon, an RFP arrived at her desk. The due date was Friday at noon—four days away. Karen's boss asked whether she would have time to respond to the RFP and craft a 50-page bid by the due date. She currently had five other bids in process. Although she couldn't forsake these other bids, she still agreed to take on the extra work. The question she posed to herself was how she should proceed. Her decision was to complete her other assignments first, and then work on the bid due Friday. Unfortunately, her other work took up until Wednesday evening to finish, so she had only all day Thursday and Friday morning to complete her assignment. What was she to do? Without panicking, she spent all day Thursday working on the RFP, left work long enough to attend her graduate class at the local university, and continued to work on the bid until 11:00 p.m. that night. Then, she went into the office at 4:30 a.m. on Friday to complete the assignment in order to meet the noon deadline, which she "easily" did.

Greg, an employment manager for a large regional discount chain, faced a perplexing issue. His firm was going to open simultaneously four new stores in a major metropolitan area. He needed to recruit 160 individuals to fill team leader positions (40 managers per store) prior to the store openings. He usually relied on his staff of eight specialists to do the hiring, and then would give his final approval of the candidates. This time, though, he decided to do his own recruiting—which was outside of his job description. He "camped out" in the city where the new stores were to be located. He scouted the competition to discern the effectiveness of their employees; after all, he hoped to recruit some of their talented staff as team leaders. He also arranged career events in area colleges and contacted recruiting agencies in the city. Much of his time was devoted to talking with managers, assistant managers, and department managers in competing and non-competing stores. Doing so helped him learn about the new market and about the individuals' potential as team leaders. Eventually, he was able to hire all the team leaders that he needed, and the stores opened fully staffed and with great fanfare—and subsequent success.

Barbara had a very pressing engagement. As an executive secretary of a university, she usually handled all the contacts for the school with respect to professors, adjunct instructors, other faculty, and staff; moreover, she answered all of the calls to the university president. Well, her pressing engagement wasn't in her bailiwick—and to top it off, the engagement was faltering on the very day it was to be held. A reception and dinner had been planned—well in advance—for the school's donors. It was to be a gala event. On the day of the event, maintenance was to clean and arrange the room for the reception and dinner. Much to her dismay, most of the maintenance personnel were off that day.

Because the event was located in a newly completed building, dirt and dust were everywhere. Consequently, Barbara seized a vacuum and went over and over the carpeting until it was spotless. Then, only two hours before the event began, Barbara noticed that several of the donors' nametags were missing from the seating arrangements in the banquet room. So, she ran to her office to type and print them. Upon returning to the room, she noticed that the champagne had not yet been poured, as the servers were not working efficiently. So she started popping the corks on champagne bottles and pouring their contents into glasses. Finally, just before the first guests arrived, her tasks were done!

DIAGNOSIS

Keith, Karen, Greg, and Barbara had to make a major decision relative to their work situation. Do they take on the assignment, despite the circumstances, or do they decline it and pass it on to another individual? Each one chose to accept the challenge, even though doing so inconvenienced (or in Keith's case, endangered) him or her. Where others might fear to tread, they did not shirk from the "opportunity."

These four individuals, as well as numerous other interviewees, took on additional responsibility so that they could be *recognized by management or their peers* and to foster *favorable perceptions* among them. Recognition, praise, and compliments can be a public proclamation about a job well done. It is an external reward that sets the exemplary employees apart from the others. Whether the comments come from managers, other employees, or even customers, the end result is distinction for the employees' taking up the gauntlet, seizing the moment when others choose to say "no," and thus feeling good about what they have done. Keith, Greg, Karen, and Barbara each received subsequent recognition— directly or indirectly (see below)—in some form for their meritorious efforts, which was the major motivation for their actions. Review the remarks of our interviewees and see the impact recognition can have on job behavior:

- "It's [the extra effort] going to reflect back on me that I'm doing a good job." – Barbara, our university executive secretary

- "You can prove…to other people around you, and possibly your boss…that I am a superb performer." – second lieutenant, National Guard

- "Doing the extra work reflects the kind of person you are." – sales manager, petroleum company

- "I enjoy the feedback, the praise of others, especially those I support." – Greg, the employment manager for the discount chain

- "I enjoy being recognized for a job well done." – Karen, our RFP support person

- "Doing extra work will make me and my firm look better." – account manager intern, advertising agency

- "I desire to do the best job I can and stand out to management." – MIS support specialist, college bookstore

- "I want people to see me visible to all people on all shifts." – general manager, call center for a large multinational brokerage firm

- "I get some recognition for doing this." – human resource manager, large multinational toy store chain

R$_X$ FOR MANAGERS

Recognition can be a powerful motivator. Notice how the four individuals in this chapter were not reluctant to take charge, to do the job, for recognition from their managers or peers. One of the least expensive means of motivating employees to do more than is expected of them is with the use of praise, recognition, or compliments. Think about how you feel when you receive commendation from others. Pretty good, huh? Well, the same applies to your employees. How much time does it take to give a pat on the back, send an e-mail or letter complimenting someone's efforts, make a phone call to say "great job," or to craft a brief notice for the house organ that chronicles an employee's superlative performance? Not much time at all. So what might managers do in using recognition? Try the following:

RECRUITING

- Look for evidence of recognition on the resume (awards, honors, achievements).

MANAGING

- Praise in public and punish in private. Recognition should be visible to others so that the commendable employee will feel unique and so that others can consider it something they can aspire to.

- As soon as you see or hear about an employee's "extra effort" performance, quickly provide some kind of recognition to the individual. The sooner praise is given after the behavior has been done, the more motivating the recognition is to the employee.

- Don't be indiscriminate in your use of praise and recognition. If you constantly praise employees for the most minor things, they eventually will see through your tactic and will no longer feel special when receiving recognition.

RETAINING

- Remember that recognition is a reward. As such, it should be used to create a distinction between employees who have done a superlative job (i.e., those going the extra mile) and those who are just performing at acceptable levels.

13

Promotion:
Opening Doors to Nirvana

"Behold the turtle. He makes progress when he sticks his neck out." – James Conan Bryant

---

Catie is one of several project assistants in a large corporate law firm with offices in several cities. She aspires some day to become an attorney, but for now she's satisfied with her current line of work. The other day she went to work with a specific goal of making good progress on one particular project whose due date was upon her. Well, even the best laid plans of mice and women can often go awry. It seems that not all of the project assistants at the firm are as energized and talented as Catie. When she arrived at work, her boss handed her five long-neglected projects that other assistants had been slow to complete, or even to begin. She did have the option of telling her boss that she was swamped with other projects, particularly the one whose due date was fast approaching. Rather than declining the extra work, however, she put it on her plate. As a result, she has been working overtime for several nights in a row, including weekends.

Tito hopes to become a stockbroker, but currently he is an intern at a brokerage firm. One day, his supervisor decided to leave early and go golfing. Prior to leaving, though, he instructed Tito to answer his phone while he was out for the remainder of the day. Soon after his boss departed, the phone rang. Oh, oh! Immediately, Tito confronted a problem. One of his supervisor's clients was in a hurry to buy a particular stock, and time was of the essence. The only problem was that Tito did not have a broker's license, so he couldn't place the trade, although he knew how. Quickly recovering his composure, he arrived at the idea of asking another broker in the office to place the trade for him. He went to one who was a friend of his boss's, explained the situation, and soon after the trade was executed. The end results were that the customer was able to purchase his shares at a good price, and his boss received a $1,000 commission on the trade. Not bad for being unable to make a trade!

Sherri works as a quality assurance employee in the kitchen of a popular restaurant. Essentially, her charge is to put the dishes on the trays for the servers. At some point she wants to move into another position at this restaurant, but currently she is learning about the various aspects of the restaurant business. As such, she chooses to wear several different hats during the day, many of which are not dictated in her job description. On any given day, for example, Sherri closely examines the cleanliness of the dishes and ensures that the proper amount of food is dished out. Also, she places the dishes on the trays for the servers, making sure that they are not overloaded nor unbalanced. Furthermore, she makes certain that the appearance of every dish a customer receives reflects culinary aesthetics. Although she does no cooking, her special touch facilitates the efforts of the chefs and the servers.

Steve is involved in banquet set-up at a racetrack restaurant. His job entails arranging the tables and chairs for large parties in the restaurant's banquet rooms. One weekend his boss accidentally scheduled a big party on Friday night and a large wedding reception the following Saturday morning. The problem confronting Steve's boss was that it would take several hours to rearrange the 800 tables and chairs from the dinner party to get them in order for the wedding reception. The boss contemplated canceling the dinner party, thus losing substantial revenue for the restaurant as well as incurring the wrath of his supervisor. Instead, Steve volunteered to come in at 1:00 a.m. on Saturday to rearrange the tables and chairs for the wedding reception. In fact, he even recruited his roommate to assist! He worked until 7:30 a.m., two hours before the wedding reception was to begin.

DIAGNOSIS

Catie, Tito, Sherri, and Steve took on extra work. Whether the issue was taking on additional projects to complete, trying to execute a stock purchase, doing more than merely placing dishes on trays, or volunteering to rearrange a banquet room, each of our employees took on the responsibility to do more than was required of him or her. Catie could have declined the extra project. Tito could have informed the customer that the trade could not be executed until his boss returned the next day. Sherri could solely do her assigned kitchen duties. And Steve did not need to volunteer, to go well out of his way in the wee hours of the night, to help rearrange the banquet room. What underlies this group's motivation, as well as some of our other interviewees', is their keen desire to ultimately *be promoted* in their respective firms.

Different rewards drive individuals to perform. A major driver for many employees is the opportunity for a promotion. A promotion signals that an employee has been doing a good job. It signifies that he or she is ready to assume increasing job responsibilities. And it is very visible to the organization, especially to one's peers and management. Going the extra mile can demonstrate that employees are team players, that they are willing to do more than is expected of them, that they have the energy and desire to go beyond the call of duty. Such efforts suggest that these people can assume additional duties, that they are capable of doing more, that they are willing to take on more work. This is the kind of stuff that promotions are made of. The words of our previously mentioned aspirants and some of our other interviewees suggest that their unusual efforts were guided by their desire for a promotion:

- "If I work hard for the firm…if I am somebody they can rely on…then I can move on up right along with the firm…they send me to law school, they may make me a partner."
  – Catie, our project assistant at the law firm

- "My efforts became apparent to management, which ultimately will provide me additional job offers in the firm."
  – branch manager, financing division of a large multinational bank

- "I wanted to demonstrate that I had potential, so that they [management] could trust me...people who actually put time into their job are the ones who move ahead." – AutoCAD drafter, engineering firm

- "I wanted to impress my boss so that I could get a permanent job with the firm." – Tito, the intern at the securities firm

- "A major reason why I do this is for advancement." – Sherri, our quality assurance employee at the restaurant

- "Such efforts will help me get promoted." – Steve, the banquet set-up employee

R$_x$ for Managers

Advancement up the ladder is not likely to happen to all employees. Some simply don't have the grist, the "right stuff," to be promoted. But those who do are often those who have walked that lonely road that is not taken by the also-rans. They assume additional responsibilities when they do not have to. They want to demonstrate to management that their current job is not sufficiently demanding and that they deserve a promotion. They demonstrate a desire to reach their potential and be rewarded for it through a promotion. So what can managers do to get the extra effort out of employees who aspire to be promoted? Try the following:

Managing

- Clearly define for employees the criteria for promotion. The criteria should be measurable and objective, not subject to capriciousness. Provide examples to help clarify for employees what they are expected to do to get a promotion.

- When promotions are made, acknowledge the promotion company wide and describe the special kinds of job behaviors the employee exhibited to bring about the promotion.

- Provide sound training for individuals before and after they are promoted. Encourage those being promoted to continue to demonstrate the kinds of extra effort that they have previously expended.

RETAINING

- Provide multiple paths for promotions, even lateral ones providing enhanced responsibilities.

14

Compensation:
Brother, Can You Spare a Dime?

*"Money isn't everything—but it's a long way ahead of what comes next." – **Edmund Stockdale***

Kevin works for a shipping company that provides packing and shipping services. Much of Kevin's job entails packing goods that are about to be shipped. Kevin had just finished his usual eight-hour shift, it was 5:00 p.m., and he was ready to go home and relax after an unusually long day packing household goods for a very large move. Just as he was about to leave for home, his boss rushed up to him and asked him if he could help pack another load that evening. A trucker had just arrived in town to pick up a shipment of household goods, and the designated packing service had dropped the ball and never packed the shipper's goods. The contract was worth a lot of money to Kevin's firm. Kevin looked around the shop to see if anyone else was available to relieve him of the assignment, since he was extremely tired. Several other employees were available to the boss, but rather than say "no," he decided to accept the boss's offer.

Sven is the manager of vending material and traffic at a large factory of a major multinational refrigeration manufacturer. He had just assumed this new position, a promotion, and decided to interview each of his employees and ask them to identify ideas or areas where they might be able to make or save money for the firm. One of his employees suggested to Sven that materials handling in the plant should be computerized. Sven thought it was a great idea, so he requested that the MIS department implement it. MIS management turned down his request cold—they didn't think that the system could be computerized. Sven, rankled, decided to program the system himself on his personal computer at home (his previous computer experience "told" him that computerization was possible). He began the programming the first week of October, worked through his Thanksgiving vacation and Christmas vacation, and by January 1st, the system was ready to go. And go it did, saving the plant considerable expense.

Debbie works as a licensed real estate assistant for an independent real estate contractor. Technically, she is his support person. Several times since she has been in this position, however, she has done numerous things that go well beyond her job description. Frequently, she has met carpet or cable installers at a recently closed house because the new owners, as well as her boss, were unable to do so. She has also stayed well beyond her normal quitting time of 5:30 p.m. to fix computer problems. In addition, she's ferried real estate contracts across town at all hours of the day and night for her boss. And her boss is likely to call her and ask her to work on Sundays, which is not one of her scheduled workdays. All of these activities manifest her expending extra effort, going the extra mile, when she literally is not required to do so.

Amy works as an associate director of a social service organization. She has many assigned duties that keep her plate full. A major fundraising event was to be held in ten days, and many loose ends remained. Amy's staff partner had been handling the event until she suddenly announced her immediate resignation. Amy was extremely concerned: "How will the fundraising event get finalized? Who will pick up the loose ends? My staff partner was the only one with intimate knowledge of the occasion; I can't just ask anyone to finish planning this crucial event." Despite her being inundated with other necessary tasks (remember her full plate), Amy decided to take on the additional responsibility of completing her former staff partner's assignment. Over the next ten days, she scrambled to make the fundraiser a success, all while attending to her other tasks.

DIAGNOSIS

Kevin, Sven, Debbie, and Amy—four employees in distinctly different kinds of work—faced decisions regarding how they should spend their time. Kevin chose to forgo his "easy chair" time after work. Sven wouldn't take "no" for an answer and ended up spending several months of his personal time ultimately improving his department's performance. Debbie continuously demonstrates that she is a Jack-of-all trades (or is that a Jackie-of-all trades?). And Amy took on a Herculean task when it might have been passed on to another employee. Not everyone would have opted for the path that these individuals chose. Clearly, alternate means of doing their jobs were readily available. Yet, each one of them was steadfast in doing more than was required of them because they were motivated by *money.*

Money is not necessarily a major driver for everyone (despite what some mangers still think). For certain employees, money's nice to have, but it's not everything—not even in a job. Nonetheless, many employees are eager to earn additional money when the conditions provide such an incentive. Going the extra mile and being rewarded for it can be reinforcing—a reward is provided for engaging in meritorious job behavior. As the aforementioned vignettes suggest, then, monetary rewards can induce one's going beyond the call of duty. Quotations from our interviewees lend support to this idea:

- "If I go above and beyond the call of duty, it makes my boss happy so I get pay raises." – Kevin, our packer

- "Our bonus system is based on the concept of going above and beyond." – Amy, the associate director

- "I do the best that I can because it is a high-paying job." – machine operator, coal company

- "Money is the 'icing on the cake.'" – Sven, our manager of vending and traffic

- "My boss has set up a bonus system based on what he sells; this makes me work harder." – Debbie, the licensed real estate assistant

- "The more you help out, the more it helps out your paycheck." – manager, health club

- "At the end of the year, you are graded on how you did; there are bonuses given out based on that grade." – sales manager, farm co-op

R_X FOR MANAGERS

Employees want to be paid for the effort they expend and the job that they do (or at least think they do). This is particularly critical when employees have walked the extra mile, gone out of their way, moved beyond the mere duties in their job description. Allocating precious income dollars thus requires a manager to be part Merlin the Magician and part Solomon. Given that monetary rewards can reinforce desirable job performance, managers can use money to try to prompt employees to go where many other employees fear to tread. How might this be accomplished? Try the following:

MANAGING

- During performance evaluations, ask employees what they have done outside their typical realm. Also, ask them what led them to engage in such behavior. This information can be used to reward high achievers.

- Ask employees what kinds of job behaviors they believe merit a pay incentive—and then reward those behaviors that you *and* they think deserve a monetary reward.

- Explain to employees how they can increase their pay by engaging in behaviors that go the extra mile.

- Identify for employees the types of "extra effort" activities that have been rewarded in the past and that are likely to be rewarded in the future.

RETAINING

- Establish a compensation system that rewards employees' extra effort.

15

Carpe Diem:
Go for It!

"We must take the current when it serves, or lose our ventures."
– William Shakespeare

There you have it. Your journey is over. You now know that our research shows that individuals working at *all* levels in virtually *all* sizes and types of organizations *can and will* rise to the occasion when circumstances call for it. Now you should know "it" when you see "it." "It" is going beyond the call of duty rather than working at the acceptable or minimum level. And there is a common denominator to all the experiences that were related to you: The workers *chose* to do what they did; they did *not* have to do what they did. And they did what they did for many reasons—upbringing, pride in work, customer satisfaction, and so on—but no one was looking over their shoulders or holding some type of threat over their heads. Each one of our interviewee workers voted "yes" to going the extra mile. Table 15-1 shows what our research revealed—the 13 drivers that impel employees to go beyond the call of duty, walk the extra mile, expend the extra effort.

Table 15-1. Why Employees Go Beyond the Call of Duty

---

1. **Internal Motivation**: Certain employees have a high need for achievement. They are simply highly motivated to create win-win situations.

2. **Initiative**: Going beyond the call of duty makes good sense to these workers. These employees don't wait until they are instructed to act.

3. **Upbringing**: Watching and listening to one's parents and guardians can instill a blueprint for life. Individuals who saw parents go the extra mile are inclined to do so.

4. **Self-Satisfaction**: Some employees take great pride in their achievements. Pride can energize individuals to put forth extra effort—and thus go the extra mile.

continued

Table 15-1. Why Employees Go Beyond the Call of Duty

5. **Empathy**: Understanding what it is like to be on the other side can motivate individuals to take action. These workers have been in a similar situation, and didn't like it.

6. **Concern**: Feeling a pledge to those they are serving leads some individuals to expend extra effort. These employees manifest a deep concern for people.

7. **Reciprocity**: Workers who feel they have been treated well by their employers go the extra mile as a way of "paying back" their organizations.

8. **Customer Acquisition and Retention**: Some employees transcend their job boundaries because they understand the importance of customer retention and new business acquisition.

9. **Customer Satisfaction**: Maintaining customer satisfaction helps build a loyal customer base. Extra effort on the part of these employees is a boost toward achieving customer satisfaction. These workers know that satisfied customers return and spread the good word.

10. **Role Modeling and Organizational Culture**: Organizations that are steeped in a tradition of going beyond the call of duty tend to reflect this in their practices. Employees in these organizations mimic the behaviors that they see in others.

11. **Recognition**: Recognition, praise, and compliments motivate these employees to put forth extra effort. And they are concerned about making a good impression on others within their organization.

12. **Promotion**: The opportunity for a promotion motivates these employees to assume greater responsibilities when needed. Such behavior suggests to management that these individuals are ready to assume a more responsible position.

13. **Compensation**: Last, but certainly not least, certain workers go beyond the call of duty in hopes of receiving financial rewards from their organization.

Admittedly, employees make their own decisions about whether they choose to go beyond the call of duty. Nonetheless, managers can definitely influence whether their workers opt to do so. Managers essentially have two related approaches to engendering "an extra effort" mentality in their organizations: (1) they can bring individuals into the organization who possess the drivers and (2) they can bring the drivers to life. How are these two approaches implemented? Through the use of six different avenues:

1. *Recruiting*: Managers should hire individuals who possess at least one of the 13 drivers. Various alternatives exist to help managers determine whether applicants have a desired driver.

2. *Training*: Several of the drivers can be instilled or enhanced in employees through training interventions. Certain drivers can be instilled in employees through the use of role playing, lectures, group discussions, and the like.

3. *Job Design*: How a job is designed can have a dramatic influence on how well employees do their jobs. Managers can provide jobs with certain characteristics that can activate certain drivers within employees.

4. *Manager Interaction*: The manner in which managers interact with their employees can contribute to whether employees are influenced by certain drivers. Thus, the nature of the contact managers have with their employees can affect whether those individuals choose to go beyond the call of duty.

5. *Company Policies*: Organizations have within their means the ability to foster employees' going the extra mile. The existence (or absence) of certain policies can facilitate emergence of some of the 13 drivers in employees.

6. *Philosophy/Inculcation*: Managers can take actions to instill in employees certain beliefs or precepts that permeate the organization. Through such efforts, managers may awaken or enhance one or a number of drivers in employees.

In essence, then, managers can create the "right" culture in which employees will be energized to go beyond the call of duty. Table 15-2 shows which of the foregoing six efforts can enliven a specific driver in employees. Moreover, specific actions managers can take vis-à-vis a given driver are provided. This summary table allows managers to (1) think about which driver(s) is (are) most critical in their particular situation and then (2) quickly determine what action(s) to take to stimulate that (those) driver(s) in employees.

Table 15-2. Summary of What Managers Can Do to Get Employees to Go Beyond the Call of Duty

Employee Drivers	Managerial Actions					
	RECRUITING	MANAGING			RETAINING	
	Recruiting	Training	Job Design	Manager Interaction	Company Policies	Philosophy/Inculcation
Internal Motivation	Recruit individuals with high energy; identify them with psychological tests or via interview.		Design jobs so employees are provided job variety, autonomy, and feedback.			Explain benefits of "just do it" behavior and downside of absence of such behavior.
Initiative	Recruit individuals that initiate ideas and projects on their own or look for ways to improve work processes.	Identify problem areas that may arise; instruct employees to correct such situations when they arise.	Empower employees to take action when necessary.	Model "just do it" behavior for employees. Don't penalize employees for taking risks.		
Upbringing	Ask applicants about their backgrounds and how they spent time when growing up; ask what beliefs were instilled in them and key lessons they learned.					
Self-Satisfaction	Determine in interview whether pride is an applicant's "hot button."	Illustrate to employees how their job fits in with or plays a critical role in the organization.	Provide adequate job latitude so employees can solve their problems.			Help employees realize that their job is not merely a means to an end.

Managerial Actions

Employee Drivers	RECRUITING	MANAGING			RETAINING	
	Recruiting	Training	Job Design	Manager Interaction	Company Policies	Philosophy/Inculcation
Empathy	Select individuals with empathy using psychological tests and interviews.	Provide empathy training through role-playing exercises.		Exhibit empathy with employees and other parties.		Explain to employees the advantages of being empathic.
Concern	Set up scenarios and ask candidates how they would address the situation; ask applicants how they view concern. Select individuals who are volunteers.			Practice caring and concern.		Encourage employees to become involved in volunteer activities.
Reciprocity				Treat employees with respect. Talk out disagreements.		Let employees know what you are providing them and why.
Customer Acquisition and Retention		Illustrate to employees how they fit into the organization and their impact on profits. Provide examples of job behavior that create customer satisfaction.		Treat customers with respect.		Inform employees about the importance of satisfying customers.

continued

Table 15-2. Summary of What Managers Can Do to Get Employees to Go Beyond the Call of Duty

Employee Drivers	Managerial Actions					
	RECRUITING	MANAGING			RETAINING	
	Recruiting	Training	Job Design	Manager Interaction	Company Policies	Philosophy/Inculcation
Customer Satisfaction		Show employees how they can garner customer satisfaction by providing a high level of service.	Empower employees to take action and provide a high level of service; give them necessary resources to carry out the action.	Ask employees what makes them satisfied customers; suggest that such behavior may be pertinent to their job situations.	Have an incentive program that rewards employees for engaging in unusual behavior that engenders customer satisfaction.	Inform employees about the importance of satisfying customers.
Role Modeling/ Organizational Culture		Assign new employees their own mentor from whom they can learn desired job behavior.		Continually demonstrate the job behavior that you want employees to exhibit; avoid modeling inappropriate behavior.		Follow a "practice what you preach" philosophy.
Recognition	Look for evidence of recognition on the applicant's resume or application.			Provide recognition shortly after desirable behavior has been exhibited. Praise in public, punish in private.	Create a system that identifies what kinds of job behaviors will be recognized.	

Managerial Actions

Employee Drivers	RECRUITING	MANAGING			RETAINING	
	Recruiting	Training	Job Design	Manager Interaction	Company Policies	Philosophy/Inculcation
Promotion		Provide training before and after employees are promoted.		Clearly define for employees the promotion criteria; use measurable, objective criteria. Indicate the kind of special behaviors that can lead to promotions.	Provide multiple paths for promotions, even for lateral ones.	
Compensation		Explain how employees can increase their pay by engaging in extra effort.		Identify the types of "extra effort" activities that have been and will be rewarded. Ask employees what led them to expend extra effort.	Establish a compensation system that rewards extra effort.	

Two actual case studies illustrate how managers can determine which drivers are especially salient to their situation and what actions can induce those drivers in employees. In the first case, a manufacturer of agricultural chemicals lost a large customer— annual sales exceeding one million dollars—to a competitor. The primary reason was price. What is of most concern to the company is that the customer had a long-standing relationship with the firm and switched suppliers for literally pennies a ton. Discussions with the salesperson involved revealed that his company does not give its sales force enough latitude in pricing decisions when orders exceed a certain range, which this potential sale did. In hindsight, both the sales manager and the salesperson opined that their competitor's price would have been met in a timely manner (i.e., not requiring higher-level attention). Furthermore, research with other salespeople revealed that other accounts have been lost under similar circumstances. Obviously, when so much revenue is at stake, the sales force must feel impelled to "just do it." "Just do it," is the critical driver in this situation that could have prevented losing these accounts. Hindsight is 20/20, but by instructing salespeople on how to handle price negotiations in the future, empowering them to take action to keep customers, and removing barriers to action (such as "fear"), this agricultural chemicals supplier can ensure that this situation is not repeated.

Let's look at the next case. This situation involves a large regional bank, which is losing customers to smaller community banks. Exit interviews with customers reveal that the major reason they are leaving is dissatisfaction with service. Thus, the bank has decided that initiatives must be taken to increase customer service. Several performance drivers are particularly relevant to this situation: pride, retaining customers and generating new business, maintaining customer satisfaction, and role modeling/organizational culture. First, managers must illustrate to customer contact personnel that they are the critical link in the transaction—in service organizations, customer contact people (e.g., bank tellers) are often equated with the service itself (i.e., the tellers *are* the bank). Training programs and mentoring are the best ways to elicit desired behaviors in employees. Second, employees need to understand which actions satisfy customers and the impact of these actions on profits. Finally, employees must be given the necessary resources, tools, and incentives that will motivate them to engage in exceptional efforts that satisfy customers.

Several important lessons for workers and managers alike can be gleaned from our research. Seriously ponder the following findings:

- Managers can increase the likelihood of employees performing beyond the call of duty by recruiting candidates that possess one or more of the attributes described in the research.

- *All* workers can rise to the occasion. All individuals we interviewed, at some point in their working lives, went above and beyond the call of duty when the situation called for it.

- Many factors motivate workers to put forth such meritorious effort. Money and promotions are indeed important, but just as important are nonfinancial factors such as internal motivation and empathy.

- All workers can look within themselves and draw upon those factors that motivate them to go the extra mile. It isn't going to be the same factor or set of factors for every individual, but everyone has some internal force driving him or her to perform.

- Managers can help workers go the extra mile by developing a culture in which workers want to do more than merely show up for work and execute the requirements of their job description. By creating the right conditions where all employees are able to do their best work, managers enable workers to look within and identify and act on those things that motivate them to perform beyond the call of duty.

Now, go for it!

INDEX